WATTS ON WEALTH

TAX AND INVESTMENT STRATEGIES
FOR CONFIDENCE IN RETIREMENT

J. Barry Watts | WealthCare Corporation

Copyright © 2024 by J. Barry Watts and Advisors Excel, LLC.

All rights reserved. No part of this publication may be reproduced, distributed, or transmitted in any form or by any means, including photocopying, recording, or other electronic or mechanical methods, without the prior written permission of the publisher, except in the case of brief quotations embodied in critical reviews and certain other noncommercial uses permitted by copyright law. For permission requests, write to the publisher at the address below. These materials are provided to you by J. Barry Watts for informational purposes only, and J. Barry Watts and Advisors Excel, LLC expressly disclaim any and all liability arising out of or relating to your use of the same. The provision of these materials does not constitute legal or investment advice and does not establish an attorney-client relationship between you and J. Barry Watts. No tax advice is contained in these materials. You are solely responsible for ensuring the accuracy and completeness of all materials as well as the compliance, validity, and enforceability of all materials under any applicable law. The advice and strategies found within may not be suitable for every situation. You are expressly advised to consult with a qualified attorney or other professional in making any such determination and to determine your legal or financial needs. No warranty of any kind, implied, expressed, or statutory, including but not limited to the warranties of title and non-infringement of third-party rights, is given with respect to this publication.

J. Barry Watts, WealthCare Corporation
2847 S. Ingram Mill, Suite B 100
Springfield, Mo. 65804
wealthcarecorp.com

Book layout ©2022 Advisors Excel, LLC

Watts on Wealth/J. Barry Watts

ISBN 9798327047013

J. Barry Watts is a tax strategist, retirement designer and the founder of the WealthCare Corporation a firm that specializes in helping business owners and retirees reduce income taxes, often by six figures or more, while designing retirement strategies customized to suit the individual needs of each client. Through American Tax Strategies, LLC, they provide compliance and tax planning designed to reduce income tax liability, and also provide retirement income planning for every year of retirement. Through WealthCare Asset Management, LLC, an SEC registered investment advisory firm, Watts and his team of advisors help individuals invest their tax savings and pursue investment strategies individually customized to each client.

The contents of this book are provided for informational purposes only and are not intended to serve as the basis for any financial decisions. Any tax, legal, or estate planning information is general in nature. Please remember that converting an employer plan account to a Roth IRA is a taxable event. Increased taxable income from the Roth IRA conversion may have several consequences. Be sure to consult with a qualified tax advisor before making any decisions regarding your IRA. It should not be construed as legal or tax advice. Always consult an attorney or tax professional regarding the applicability of this information to your unique situation.

Information presented is believed to be factual and up-to-date, but we do not guarantee its accuracy, and it should not be regarded as a complete analysis of the subjects discussed. All expressions of opinion are those of the author as of the date of publication and are subject to change. Content should not be construed as personalized investment advice, nor should it be interpreted as an offer to buy or sell any securities mentioned. A financial advisor should be consulted before implementing any of the strategies presented.

Investing involves risk, including the potential loss of principal. No investment strategy can guarantee a profit or protect against loss in periods of declining values. Any references to protection benefits or guaranteed/lifetime income streams refer only to fixed insurance products, not securities or investment products. Insurance and annuity product guarantees are backed by the financial strength and claims-paying ability of the issuing insurance company. WealthCare is not affiliated with the U.S. government or any governmental agency.

Any names used in the examples in this book are hypothetical only and do not represent actual clients.

To Kelly, my everything.

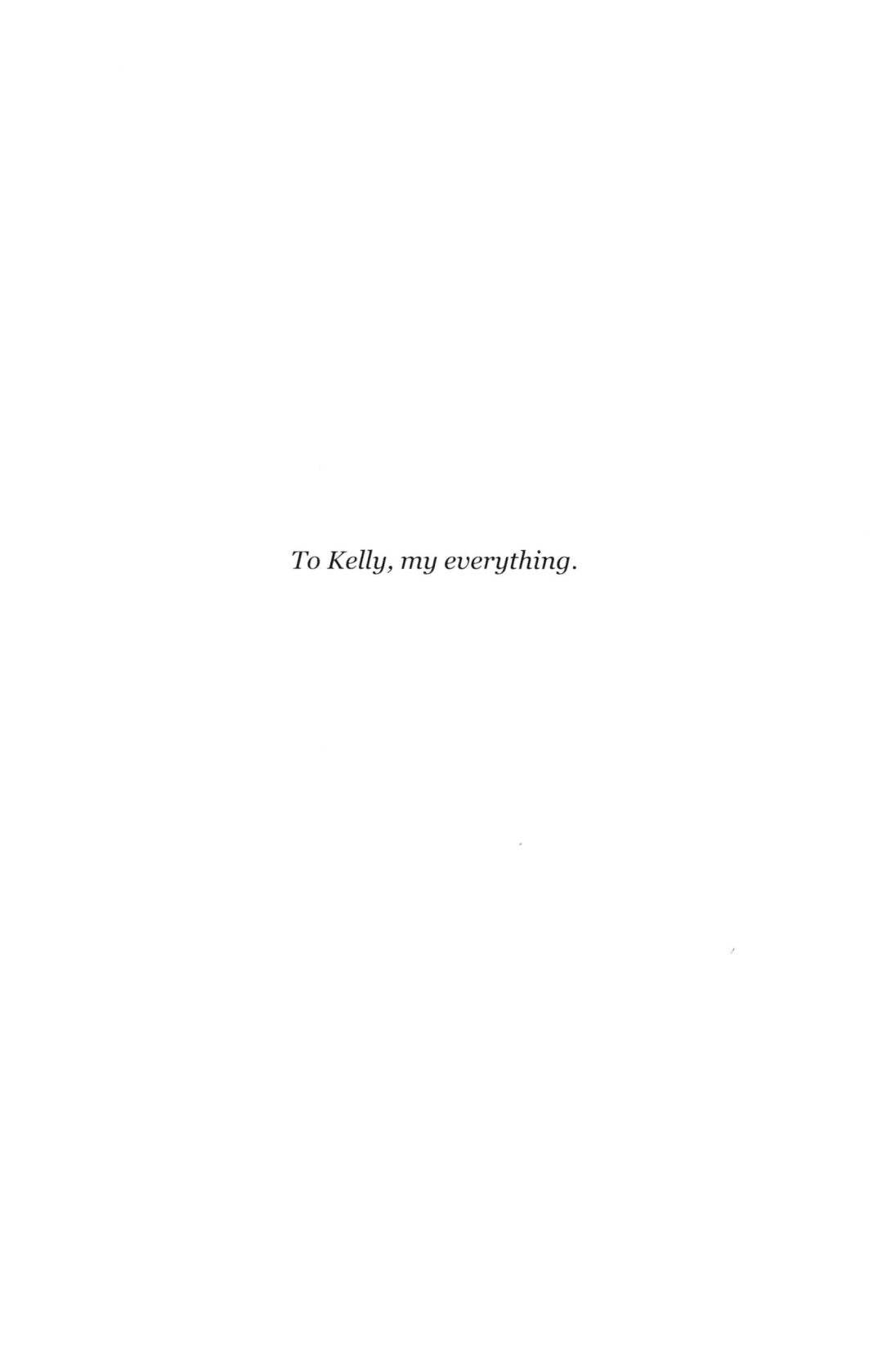

Table of Contents

The Importance of Planning i
Longevity 1
Taxes 23
Market Volatility 33
Retirement Income 41
Social Security 59
401(k)s, IRAs, and Roth IRAs 75
Annuities 87
Estate and Legacy Planning Strategies 97
Women Retire Too 109
Long-Term Care 123
Finding a Financial Professional 131
About the Author 139

PREFACE
The Importance of Planning

I was fifteen years old when my grandfather passed away unexpectedly, sending shockwaves through our family. He was the patriarch who ruled with an iron fist wrapped in a velvet glove of love for his children and grandchildren.

I was there when he died, suddenly on the back stoop of the post office in our little town, and watched as my uncle and my girlfriend's father labored aggressively to save him but to no avail. Just the night before, we'd gathered at the house he shared with my Granny and celebrated my dad's birthday. Little did we know, it would be our final meal together.

As everyone received a piece of chocolate cake, the family engaged in conversation. My grandfather shared how content he felt with everything going well in life. His children and grandchildren lived nearby and frequently visited. Also, he had $100,000 safely tucked away in the bank. What more could a man ask for?

Yet the next day, after he suddenly passed, I found myself concerned about my grandmother. I asked my mom, "What will Granny do?" I thought she might move in with us and, a bit selfishly, wondered if she would take my room.

Mom reassured me that Granny would continue living in her own house, but it left me wondering, who would take care of her? She seldom ever drove, relying on my grandfather to take her wherever she needed to go.

Clearly, times were different — enough so that $100,000 was indeed a significant amount of money not only to have deposited in the bank, but also to cover retirement expenses.

My grandfather happened to be a remarkably significant mentor in my life as a kid growing up in tiny Galena, Missouri, the Stone County seat for a county that borders on Arkansas. He taught me to drive when I was eight years old. We lived in a house that was on one of his farms about a mile from where he lived. Every Saturday morning, I would eagerly wait for him to swing by in his green 1972 pickup, and we would feed hay to his cattle. First, he let me behind the wheel to go down the driveway, and before long, I began tooling down the highway.

It's just what you did back in the day in rural America, particularly within our picturesque valley where the Railey Creek meets the James River. I would frequently see my grandfather several times a week. The summer before he died, we spent a lot of time fishing together. He meant a lot to me, and I missed him.

The vivid memory of my grandfather's death never faded. It became a moment emblazoned on my soul in a way. It was a life-altering event that made me realize the importance of caring for our loved ones and securing their future. It was a foundational experience that steered me toward a career in financial planning.

****

My career path took a different turn at the outset. Right out of college, I detoured from my undergraduate training in economics and became a pastor, first in a rural church outside Columbia, Missouri, and then starting a church in my living room that grew to several hundred people and had a significant impact on our city. In my pastoral counseling room, one of the consistent themes was marital tension couples experience, often because of money — typically the lack of it. So the financial concern with my Granny, and the money concerns of my parishioners provided a natural on-ramp into the financial planning field as I shifted vocational gears a few years later.

Like most, I started out in the financial industry selling insurance and investment products. That's where the job opportunities were. But I wanted to help people with financial planning. That led me to eventually become a Certified Financial Planner and start my own company independent from all the Wall Street firms. Eventually, I recognized the unmet need for tax advice and returned to school to obtain crucial tax strategy planning tools. But the roots of my career trace back to that experience with Granny and Grandad. That experience blossomed into the career I know today.

I started early. In 1984, while in my junior year of study at the University of Missouri, my dad encouraged me to look into the insurance industry.

In those pre-internet days, you got a license by reading a massive textbook roughly the size of an old Sears catalog. I dove in, and a couple of weeks later, I took my test. At the age of twenty, I became a licensed insurance broker. It was a bit overwhelming at first, forcing me to rely on my ingenuity to attract clients.

Back then, newspapers were well-staffed and attempted to generate a vast array of content. Also, everyone still had a landline, and most of their phone numbers could be accessed through public listings. So, I would read the birth announcements in the paper and then, armed with a phone book, called on proud, new parents. I informed parents how to secure a college fund for their little ones using life insurance. Many of them agreed to meet with me.

Although I figured out on the fly what to do and say during those appointments, I never let it stress me out. One day, I stumbled upon an experienced colleague who took me under his wing. He helped me create a sales kit and armed me with a handy flip chart. Together, we successfully signed up parents to invest in life insurance policies that would benefit their children's education. Looking back, there were better ways to do it, but I was just starting out. What did I know?

One of the gifts God has given me is the ability to take a situation and translate it into the unique language of whoever I am talking to. I once found myself explaining a tax and investment strategy to a farmer in my office. I could see his eyes glazing over as I tried to explain this concept that wasn't his everyday "heart" language, so I pivoted and told him a story he recognized about two breeds of cows — one that sells for top dollar, and another breed whose price is often closer to the bottom-of-the-barrel.

As I told him that story, I saw his eyes light up as he made the connection between the bottom-of-the-barrel investments he owned, the top-end investments I wanted him to switch to, and the tax implications of making the switch. I really enjoy explaining tax and investment concepts in the language and situations relatable to my clients' everyday working lives. It tickles me when I can see they get it.

****

After nine years working in ministry, I leaned back on my economics degree and insurance experience. Right out of college, several of my peers had entered the brokerage industry, it seemed like a natural fit. I joined the largest member firm of the New York Stock Exchange, where I quickly learned the ins and outs of stocks, bonds, and other financial instruments.

It was all coming together. My gifts of preaching made me a natural teacher. My pastoral experience counseling and organizing aligned perfectly with becoming a financial planner. Unfortunately, the big-box Wall Street firm didn't seem to appreciate those gifts and passions. They wanted me to generate commissions brokering stocks, bonds, and mutual funds.

I felt called to a deeper purpose than selling investments. My time as a pastor taught me to convey God's message and engage a congregation on Sunday, a community socially, and individuals personally regarding the decisions they needed to make.

Some of my conversations as a pastor involved communicating difficult truths, and holding people to high standards they might initially resist. It's your role to lead people through failures and toward strategies and adjustments that can help them flourish. Remember, Jesus' sacrifice on the cross has already paved the way, erasing our past mistakes and opening the path to establish a relationship with God.

Similarly, when clients seek financial advice, you acknowledge their past missteps without dwelling on their shortcomings. The focus must shift to the present and the future, forging a path towards financial growth. Ultimately, the parallels between the roles of a financial advisor and a pastor are strikingly similar, whether providing financial guidance or spiritual support.

While the Word of God is uncompromising in what it requires, I discovered that with financial planning, flexibility is vital because everyone is different in their stories and aspirations. This is where the retirement planning process begins. Not so much with assets accumulated but how those assets shape the future you want in retirement.

Our WealthCare team wants you to focus on your retirement vision. We want to help empower you to make informed decisions customized to your circumstances. By factoring all the necessary elements outlined in this book, we believe you can experience great clarity with your retirement decisions, bringing you great joy in your retirement experience.

Potential Risks to Your Ideal Retirement

Ever feel like life gets in the way and prevents you from doing things you shouldn't ignore? I think if we're honest with ourselves, we've all put off obligations we know are important. In your case, you may be reading this book because it's time to get serious about financial planning and, specifically, devising a way to ideally prepare for retirement. A retirement plan should be based on more components than just your investments or your finances. The preparation of that strategy begins with your desires, ambitions, and goals for this fulfilling season of life.

There's no such thing as a silly question — not when one of the most common questions we hear from folks regarding retirement is, "Am I going to be okay?" It often seems people are reluctant to meet with financial professionals because they worry they might sound uneducated. However, it's understandable for you to be a novice when it comes to financial issues and retirement concerns. You've been busy with your lives and your careers. Time spent away from work has meant time spent being around those you love and engaging in the activities you enjoy. Retirement provides the opportunity to do even more of that, while not fretting over work obligations.

Concerns people have about what they may encounter during retirement can be far-reaching and still perfectly legitimate. For a quick snapshot, I want to provide a brief sampling of wide-ranging issues that can come up during discussions about what to potentially brace for in retirement. This book will touch on many of these issues in further detail.

Politics: A presidential election often stirs emotions regarding potential effects on the economy. Investors grow anxious about how a new president can influence market returns. It's Congress, however, that establishes tax laws and passes spending bills. Yet the president can indirectly affect the economy and the stock market in various ways such as the appointment of policymakers, development of international relations, and influential sway on new legislation.

Taxes: An example of a president's influence can be cited in signature legislation passed during Donald Trump's presidency, the Tax Cuts and Jobs Act of 2017. However, our tax system remains progressive, so the more you earn, the higher the tax rate within each tax bracket of subsequently higher income. A thorough understanding of tax regulations can be crucial. A financial professional can help identify potential issues a tax professional can help solve.

Inflation: General increases in the prices of goods and services, often measured using the consumer price index (CPI) often stem from fluctuations in real demand for goods and services. Inflation can discourage investment, as well as shortages in goods. A retiree's income can be impacted by the effect inflation can have on a fixed budget. The value of currency decreases because inflation erodes purchasing power.

Cybersecurity: Think you'll give up your smartphone in retirement? No way, right? It's here to stay, along with other intellectual gadgetry, including devices that have not been patented or invented yet. Retirees are becoming more tech-savvy, yet they can also be more trusting, which can be problematic when responding to potential scammers by phone, text, or email. Cybercrime often uses technology to target potential victims. Scammers, much like technology, figure to only grow more sophisticated over time.

CHAPTER 1

Longevity

You would think the prospect of the grave would loom more frightening as we age, yet many retirees say their number one concern is actually running out of money in their twilight years.[1] Unfortunately, this concern is justified because of one significant factor: We're living longer.

According to the Social Security Administration's 2011 Trustee Report, in 1950, the average life expectancy for a sixty-five-year-old man was seventy-eight, and the average for a sixty-five-year-old woman was eighty-one.[2] In the 2023 Trustees Report issued by the SSA, those averages were eighty-three and eighty-six, respectively.[3]

The bottom line of many retirees' budget woes comes down to this: They just didn't plan to live so long. Now, when we are younger and in our working years, that's not something we necessarily see as a bad thing; don't some people fantasize about living forever or, at least, reaching the ripe old age of 100?

However, with a longer lifespan, we face a few snags as we retire. Our resources are finite — we only have so much money to provide income — but our lifespans can be unpredictably

---

[1] Brett Arends. MarketWatch. June 5, 2023. "Americans are 'more afraid of running out of money than death'"
https://www.marketwatch.com/story/americans-are-more-afraid-of-running-out-money-than-death-ee5e22e9
[2] Social Security Administration. 2024. "Actuarial Publications: Cohort Life Expectancy" https://www.ssa.gov/oact/TR/2011/lr5a4.html
[3] Social Security Administration. 2023. "Period Life Expectancy — 2023 OASDI Trustees Report" https://www.ssa.gov/OACT/TR/2023/lr5a4.html

long, perhaps longer than our resources allow. Also, longer lives don't necessarily equate with healthier lives. The longer you live, the more money you will likely need to spend on health care, even excluding long-term care needs like nursing homes.

You will also run into inflation. If you don't plan to live another twenty-five years but end up doing so, inflation at an average of 3 percent will approximately double the price of goods over that time period.

Because we don't necessarily get to have our cake and eat it, too, our collective increased longevity hasn't necessarily increased the healthy years of our lives. Typically, our life-extending care most widely applies to the time in our lives when we will need more care in general. Think of common situations like a pacemaker at eighty-five, or cancer treatment at seventy-eight.

"Wow, Barry," I can hear you say. "Way to start with the good news first."

I know, I've painted a grim picture, but all I'm concerned about here is cost. It's hard to put a dollar sign on life, but that is essentially what we're talking about when discussing longevity and finances. Living longer isn't a bad thing; it just costs more, and one key to a sound retirement strategy is preparing for it in advance.

All the work you put in throughout your career hopefully leads to a long, prosperous life. But what if, despite your best efforts, you run out of money? Increased longevity means difficulty if you haven't planned for how you can support yourself throughout your retirement years, which statistics tell us may likely end in escalating healthcare costs during the final years of your life.

You don't want to end life's journey unable to get the care you or your spouse may need. By taking charge of your financial situation as soon as possible, you can potentially extend your funds for an additional fifteen or twenty glorious years. Not only does this ensure your well-being and security, but it could also allow you to leave a lasting legacy for your loved ones.

So why on earth would you ignore these potentially crucial matters stemming from longevity? Paying attention to them can only result in a better, easier life for you and the potential for a brighter future for your children. Living longer may be more expensive, but it can also prove meaningful when you plan for it.

Retiring Early

A key part of planning for retirement revolves around retirement income. After all, retirement is cutting the cord that tethers you to your employer — and your monthly check. However, that check often comes with many other benefits, particularly health care. Health care is often the thing that can unexpectedly put dreams for an early retirement on hold. Some employers offer health benefits to their retired workers, but that number has declined drastically over the past several decades.

In 1988, among employers who offered health benefits to their workers, 66 percent offered health benefits to their retirees. That number has since dwindled to 21 percent.[4] So, with employer-offered retirement health benefits on the wane, this becomes a major point of concern for anyone who is looking to retire, particularly those who are looking to retire before age sixty-five, when they would become eligible for Medicare coverage.

Fidelity estimates that the average retired couple at age sixty-five will need approximately $315,000 for health care expenses in retirement, not including long-term care.[5] Do you think it's likely that cost will decrease?

---

[4] Henry J. Kaiser Family Foundation. October 27, 2022. "2022 Employer Health Benefits Survey" https://www.kff.org/report-section/ehbs-2022-section-11-retiree-health-benefits/
[5] Fidelity. June 21, 2023. "How to plan for rising health care costs" https://www.fidelity.com/viewpoints/personal-finance/plan-for-rising-health-care-costs

Even if you are working until age sixty-five or have plans to cover your health expenses until that point, I often have clients who incorrectly assume Medicare is their golden ticket to cover all expenses. That is simply not the case.

Retiring Later

Planning for a long life in retirement partly depends on when you retire. While many people end up retiring earlier than they anticipated — due to injuries, layoffs, family crises, and other unforeseen circumstances — continuing to work past age sixty (and even sixty-five) is still a viable option for others and can be an excellent way to help establish financial confidence in retirement.

There are many reasons for this. For one, you obviously still earn a paycheck and the benefits accompanying it. Medical coverage and beefing up your retirement accounts with further savings can be significant by themselves, but continuing to generate income should also keep you from dipping into your retirement funds, further allowing them the opportunity to grow.

Additionally, for many workers, their nine-to-five job is more than just clocking in and out. Having a sense of purpose can keep us active physically, mentally, and socially. That kind of activity and level of engagement may also help stave off many of the health problems that plague retirees. Avoiding a sedentary life is one of the advantages of staying plugged into the workforce, if possible.

I estimate that more than half of our clients take on some form of work after "retiring." It could be as a consultant working in the same field as before, or even something completely different.

Kiddingly, I'll share with my clients that when I retire, I want to drive the shuttle bus at Silver Dollar City. I can already recite the lines the driver says to those headed to the theme park. When they were little, my daughters' favorite ride at Silver

Dollar City was the tram into the park. And that was prior to arriving at the gate, where you had to pay your entrance fee. What a deal for me!

I have a client who's doing something similar. After retiring from an agricultural manufacturing company, he now drives golfers from the Springfield airport to the golf courses near Branson.

Frankly, there are many pursuits clients have explored in retirement that help them earn a little spending money and continue to engage with people. One happens to be a member of our WealthCare staff who retired after twenty-five years, only to find that after being away for several months, retirement wasn't what she expected. She missed the interaction she enjoyed with our staff and clients.

One client jokes that she missed interacting with criminals. She works as a court clerk processing the miscreants through the court system in her little town.

When I think about my own retirement, I don't know if I'll ever fully walk away. I might consider reducing my hours, working with a select group of clients, and only participating in activities I truly enjoy. The idea of retiring and doing nothing doesn't appeal to me. I want to stay engaged and active. Retirement is about making it what you want it to be.

Health Care

Take a second to reflect on your health care plan. Although working up to or even past age sixty-five could allow you to avoid a coverage gap between your working years and Medicare, that may not be an option for you. Even if it is, when you retire, you will need to make some decisions about what kind of insurance coverage you may need to supplement your Medicare. Are there any medical needs you have that may require coverage in addition to Medicare? Did your parents or grandparents have any inherited medical conditions you might consider using a special savings plan to cover?

These are all questions that are important to review with your financial professional so you can be sure you have enough money put aside for health care.

Long-Term Care

Longevity means the need for long-term care is statistically more likely to happen. If you intend to pass on a legacy, planning for long-term care is paramount, since most estimates project nearly 70 percent of Americans who reach age sixty-five will need some type of it.[6] However, this may be one of the biggest, most stressful pieces of longevity planning I encounter in my work. For one thing, who wants to talk about the point in their lives when they may feel the most limited? Who wants to dwell on what will happen if they can no longer toilet, bathe, dress, or feed themselves?

I get it; this is a less-than-fun part of planning. But a little bit of preparation now can go a long way!

When it comes to your longevity, just like with your goals, one of the important things to do is sit and dream. It may not be the fun, road-trip-to-the-Grand-Canyon kind of dreaming, but you can spend time envisioning how you want your twilight years to look.

For instance, if it is important for you to live in your home for as long as possible, who will provide for the day-to-day fixes and to-dos of housework if you become ill? Will you set aside money for a service, or do you have relatives or friends nearby whom you could comfortably allow to help you? Do you prefer in-home care over a nursing home or assisted living? This could be a good time to discuss the possibility of moving into a retirement community versus staying where you are or whether it's worth moving to another state and leaving relatives behind.

---

[6] Claire Samuels. A Place for Mom. September 13, 2023. "Long-Term Care Statistics: A Portrait of Americans in Assisted Living, Nursing Homes, and Skilled Nursing Facilities" https://www.aplaceformom.com/senior-living-data/articles/long-term-care-statistics

These are all important factors to discuss with your spouse and children, as *now* is the right time to address questions and concerns. For instance, is aging in place more important to one spouse than the other? Are the friends or relatives who live nearby emotionally, physically, and financially capable of helping you for a time if you face an illness?

Many families I meet with find these conversations very uncomfortable, particularly when children discuss nursing home care with their parents. A knee-jerk reaction for many is to promise they will care for their aging parents. This is noble and well-intentioned, but there needs to be an element of realism here. Does "help" from an adult child mean they stop by and help you with laundry, cooking, home maintenance, and bills? Or does it mean they move you into their spare room when you have hip surgery? Are they prepared to help you use the restroom and bathe if that becomes difficult for you to do on your own?

I don't mean to discourage families from caring for their own; this can be a profoundly admirable relationship when it works out. However, I've seen families put off planning for late-in-life care based on a tenuous promise that the adult children would care for their parents, only to watch as the support system crumbles. Sometimes, this is because the assumed caregiver hasn't given serious thought to the preparation they would need, both in a formal sense and regarding their personal physical, emotional, and financial commitments. This is often also because we can't see the future: Alzheimer's disease and other maladies of old age can exact a heavy toll. When a loved one reaches the point where they are at risk of wandering away or needing help with two or more activities of daily living, it can be more than one person or a family can realistically handle.

If you know what you want, communicate with your family about both the best-case and worst-case scenarios. Then, hope for the best, and plan for the worst.

Realistic Cost of Care

Included in your planning should be a consideration for the cost of long-term care. The potential costs for such care and treatment can be underestimated, especially by those who have maintained robust health and find it difficult to envision future declines in their condition.

Another piece of planning for long-term care costs is anticipating inflation. It's common knowledge that prices have been and keep rising, which can lower your purchasing power on everything from food to medical care. Long-term care is a big piece of the inflation-disparity pie.

While local costs vary from state to state, the following table shows the national median for various forms of long-term care (plus projections that account for a 3 percent annual inflation, so you can see what I am referencing):[7]

---

[7] Nationwide. 2024. "Compare Long-term Care costs from state to state" https://nationwidefinancialltcmap.hvsfinancial.com/

Long-Term Care Costs: Inflation				
	Informal Care	Home Care	Assisted Living	Nursing Home (semi-private room)
Annual 2024	$42,037	$33,621	$60,874	$113,522
Annual 2034	$56,495	$45,184	$81,810	$160,134
Annual 2044	$75,924	$60,723	$109,945	$225,884
Annual 2054	$102,036	$81,607	$147,757	$318,632

Fund Your Long-Term Care

One common mistake I see occurs in those who haven't planned for long-term care because they assume the government will provide everything. But that's a big misconception. The government has two health insurance programs: Medicare and Medicaid. These can greatly assist you in your health care *needs* in retirement but usually don't provide enough coverage to cover all your health care *costs* in retirement. My firm isn't a government outpost, so we don't get to make decisions regarding policy and specifics about either of these programs. I'm going to give an overview of both, but if you want to dive into the details of these programs, you can visit www.Medicare.gov and www.Medicaid.gov.

Medicare
Medicare covers those aged sixty-five and older and those who are disabled. Medicare's coverage of any nursing-home-related health issues is limited. It might cover your nursing home stay

if it is not a "custodial" stay and isn't long-term. For example, if you break a bone or suffer a stroke, stay in a nursing home for rehabilitative care, and then return home, Medicare may cover you. However, if you have developed dementia or are looking to move to a nursing facility because you can no longer bathe, dress, toilet, feed yourself, or take care of your hygiene, etc., then Medicare is not going to pay for your nursing home costs.[8]

You can enroll in Medicare anytime during the three months before and three months after your sixty-fifth birthday. Miss your enrollment deadline, and you could risk paying increased premiums for the rest of your life.[9] In addition to prompt enrollment, there are a few other things to think about when it comes to Medicare, not least among them being the need to understand the different "parts," what they do, and what they don't cover.

Part A

Medicare Part A is what you might think of as "classic" Medicare. Hospital care, some types of home health care, and major medical care fall under this. While most enrollees pay nothing for this service (as they likely paid into the system for at least ten years), you might have to, based on either work history or delayed signup. In 2024, the highest premium is $505 per month, and a hospital stay does have a deductible — $1,632.[10] Also, if you have a hospital stay that surpasses sixty days, you could be looking at additional costs; keep in mind, Medicare doesn't pay for long-term care and services.

---

[8] Medicare. 2024. "What Part A covers" https://www.medicare.gov/what-medicare-covers/what-part-a-covers
[9] Medicare. 2024. "When can I sign up for Medicare?" https://www.medicare.gov/basics/get-started-with-medicare/sign-up/when-can-i-sign-up-for-medicare
[10] Centers for Medicare & Medicaid Services. October 12, 2023. "2024 Medicare Parts A & B Premiums and Deductibles" https://www.cms.gov/newsroom/fact-sheets/2024-medicare-parts-b-premiums-and-deductibles?ref=biztoc.com

Part B

Medicare Part B is an essential piece of wrap-around coverage for Medicare Part A. It helps pay for doctor visits and outpatient services. This also comes with a price tag: Although the Part B annual deductible is only $240 in 2024, you will still pay 20 percent of all costs after that, with no limit on out-of-pocket expenses. The Part B monthly premium for 2024 ranges from the standard amount of $174.70 to $594.[11]

Part C

Medicare Part C (more commonly known as a Medicare Advantage plan) is an alternative to a combination of Parts A, B, and sometimes D. Administered through private insurance companies, these have a variety of costs and restrictions, and they are subject to the specific policies and rules of the issuing carrier.

Part D

Medicare Part D is also offered through a private insurer and is supplemental to Parts A and B, as its primary purpose is to cover prescription drugs. Like any private insurance plan, Part D has its quirks and rules that vary from insurer to insurer.

The Donut Hole

Even with a "Part D" in place, you may still have a coverage gap between what your Part D private drug insurance pays for your prescription and what basic Medicare pays. In 2024, the coverage gap is $5,030, meaning that after you meet your private prescription insurance limit, you will spend no more

---

[11] Ibid.

than 25 percent of your drug costs out-of-pocket before Medicare kicks in to pay for more prescription drugs.[12]

Note: In the donut hole, you pay up to 25 percent out of pocket for all covered medications. You leave the donut hole once you've spent $8,000 out of pocket for covered drugs in 2024. 2024 is the last year for the donut hole. A $2,000 out-of-pocket cap takes effect for Medicare Part D in 2025.

Medicare Supplements

Medicare Supplement Insurance, MedSupp, Medigap, or plans labeled Medicare Part F, G, H, I, J … Known by a variety of monikers, this is just a fancy way of saying "medical coverage for those over sixty-five that picks up the tab for whatever the federal Medicare program(s) doesn't." Again, costs, limitations, etc., vary by carrier.

Does that sound like a bunch of government alphabet soup to you? It certainly does to me. And did you read the fine print? Unpredictable costs, varied restrictions, difficult-to-compare benefits, donut holes, and coverage gaps. That's par for the course with health care plans throughout our adult lives. What gives? I thought Medicare was supposed to be easier, comprehensive, and at no cost!

The truth is there is probably no stage of life when health care is easy to understand.

One of the best things you can do for yourself is to scope out the health care options early, compare costs often, and prepare for out-of-pocket expenses well in advance — decades, if possible.

I remember a couple who was in a great position to retire relatively early, with plenty of money. But one thing held them back. They worried about health care costs between the point they could retire and when they reached Medicare age. I

---

[12] Medicare. 2024. "Costs in the coverage gap" https://www.medicare.gov/drug-coverage-part-d/costs-for-medicare-drug-coverage/costs-in-the-coverage-gap

attempted to ease their concerns that health care costs could deplete their savings. Their worries were unfounded based on the assets they had amassed. Yet, instead of overcoming their concern with a logical outlook on retiring, they chose to continue working.

We even engaged in a thorough discussion of Medicare, though I understand why it's easy for people to grow confused about Medicare's layers of complexity. There are Part A, Part B, and Part D for drugs, and even Medicare Advantage (Part C). More letters exist, too, for additional services. The basics of Medicare sometimes confuse people.

You have to pay for Medicare when you retire. Money gets deducted every month from your Social Security benefit. I once had a financial professional attend one of the classes I teach, and even he didn't realize that he would have to pay for Medicare. He also didn't understand that having more money in your IRA means higher Medicare costs and potential Social Security taxation. It's important to plan wisely to avoid running out of money down the road.

I can cite members of my family when touching on the oddities of Medicare. My mother received around $1,300 in cash one year through her Medicare Advantage plan. An unusual situation resulted in the government overpaying the insurance company for my mother's Medicare Advantage. The insurance company had to refund the overcharge. Instead of repaying the excess back to the government, the insurance company sent it to my mother.

The situation is hard to understand, but I can go on and touch on another Medicare oddity affecting my wife's side of the family. My mother-in-law has a Medicare plan that prompts my wife to sit down with her every quarter of the year, sift through a catalog, and use excess benefits to buy things nobody needs or wants — items such as Apple watches and step-o-meters. Medicare just wants to send her stuff. We're always trying to find some useful items amidst this waste of government funds. It's a baffling situation. And let me tell you, it sure gets people fired up. It's a grave misuse of our taxpayer dollars.

Medicaid

Medicaid is a program the states administer, so funding, protocol, and limitations vary. Compared to Medicare, Medicaid more widely covers nursing home care, but it targets a different demographic: those with low incomes.

If you have more assets than the Medicaid limit in your state and need nursing home care, you will need to use those assets to pay for your care. You will also have a list of additional state-approved ways to use or spend some of these assets over the Medicaid limit, such as pre-purchasing burial plots and funeral expenses or paying off debts. After that, your remaining assets fund your nursing home stay until they are gone, at which point Medicaid will jump in.

Some people aren't stymied by this, thinking they will just pass on their financial assets early by gifting them to relatives, friends, and causes so they can qualify for Medicaid when they need it. However, to prevent this exact scenario, Uncle Sam has implemented what's called the "look-back period." Currently, if you enroll in Medicaid, you are subject to having the government scrutinize the last five years of your finances for large gifts or expenses that may subject you to penalties, temporarily making you ineligible for Medicaid coverage.

So, if you're planning to preserve your money for future generations and retain control of your financial resources during your lifetime, you'll probably want to prepare for the costs of longevity beyond a "government plan."

Self-Funding

One way to fund a longer life is the old-fashioned way, through self-funding. There are a variety of financial tools you can use, and they all have their pros and cons. If your assets are in low-interest financial vehicles (savings, bonds, CDs), you risk letting inflation erode the value of your dollar. If you are relying on the stock market, you have more growth potential, but you'll also want to consider the possible implications of market volatility. What if your assets take a hit? If you suffer a loss in your retirement portfolio in early or mid-retirement, you might have the option to "tighten your belt," so to speak, and cut back on discretionary spending to allow your portfolio the room to bounce back. But if you are retired and depend on income from a stock account that just hit a downward stride, what are you going to do?

HSAs
These days, you might also be able to self-fund through a health savings account (HSA) if you have access to one through a high-deductible health plan (you will not qualify to save in an HSA after enrolling in Medicare). In an HSA, any growth of your tax-deductible contributions will be tax-free, and any distributions paid out for qualified health costs are also tax-free. Long-term care expenses count as health costs, so if this is an option available to you, it is one way to use the tax advantages to self-fund your longevity. Bear in mind if you are younger than sixty-five, any money you use for non-qualified expenses will be subject to taxes and penalties, and if you are older than sixty-five, any HSA money you use for non-medical expenses is subject to income tax.

LTCI
One slightly more nuanced way to pay for longevity — specifically for long-term care — is long-term care insurance (LTCI). As car insurance protects your assets in case of a car accident and home insurance protects your assets in case something happens to your house, long-term care insurance aims to protect your assets in case you need long-term care in an at-home or nursing home situation.

As with other types of insurance, you will pay a monthly or annual premium in exchange for an insurance company paying for long-term care down the road. Typically, policies cover two to three years of care, which is adequate for an "average" situation: it's estimated that 70 percent of Americans aged sixty-five and older will need long-term care of some kind.[13]

Now, there are a few oft-cited components of LTCI that make it unattractive for some:
- Expense — LTCI can be expensive. It is generally less expensive the younger you are, but a sixty-five-year-old couple who purchased LTCI in 2023 could expect to pay a combined annual amount of $3,750 for a policy. And the annual cost only increases from there the older you are.[14]
- Limited options — LTCI may be expensive for consumers, but it can also be expensive for companies that offer it. With fewer companies willing to take on that expense, the market narrows, meaning opportunities to price shop for policies with different options or custom benefits are limited.
- If you know you need it, you might not be able to get it — Insurance companies offering LTCI are taking on a risk that you may need LTCI. That risk is the foundation of the product — you may or may not need it. If you know you will need it because you have a dementia diagnosis or another illness for which you will need long-term care, you will likely not qualify for LTCI coverage.
- Use it or lose it — If you have LTCI and are in the minority of Americans who die having never needed long-term care, all the money you paid into your LTCI policy is gone.

---

[13] Claire Samuels. A Place for Mom. September 13, 2023. "Long-Term Care Statistics: A Portrait of Americans in Assisted Living, Nursing Homes, and Skilled Nursing Facilities" https://www.aplaceformom.com/senior-living-data/articles/long-term-care-statistics

[14] American Association for Long-Term Care Insurance. 2023. "Long-Term Care Insurance Facts – Data – Statistics – 2023 Reports" https://www.aaltci.org/long-term-care-insurance/learning-center/ltcfacts-2023.php

- Possibly fluctuating rates — Your premium rate is not locked in on LTCI. Companies maintain the ability to raise or lower your premium amounts. This means some seniors face an ultimatum: Keep funding a policy at what might be a less affordable rate *or* lose coverage and let go of all the money they have paid so far.

After that, you might be thinking, "How can people possibly be interested in LTCI?" But let me repeat myself — it's anticipated that as many as 70 percent of Americans will need long-term care. And although only one in ten Americans aged fifty-five-plus has purchased LTCI, keep in mind the high cost of nursing home care. Can you afford $7,000 a month to put into nursing home care and still have enough left over to help protect your legacy? This is a genuine concern, not only because of the aforementioned statistic about long-term care needs but also because nearly a third of American seniors have some level of cognitive impairment — including 10 percent who have dementia.[15] So, not to sound like a broken record, but it is vitally important to have a plan in place to deal with longevity and long-term care, especially if you intend to leave a financial legacy.

When I started my career, our team worked with clients to obtain long-term care insurance. However, over time, long-term care insurance became increasingly expensive. Premiums would go up annually, while the benefits would often decrease. The "use it or lose it" nature of long-term care insurance discourages people. Clients would invest significant money into the policy, only to lose it if they never needed to use it.

Given these factors, I believe long-term care insurance is not advantageous. Fortunately, alternative methods to cover long-term care guarantee you'll receive your premiums back if your

---

[15] Peter Urban. AARP. November 1, 2022. "1 in 10 Older Americans Have Dementia" https://www.aarp.org/health/brain-health/info-2022/cognitive-impairment-trends-in-older-americans.html

benefits go unused. This could even be in the form of tax-free money that you can spend for yourself or pass on to your heirs.

A few relevant statistics to keep in mind:
- The longer you live, the more health care you will likely need to pay for.
- The median cost of a private nursing home room in the United States between 2022 and 2023 was $9,034 a month.[16] But keep in mind that is just the nursing home — it doesn't include other medical costs, let alone pleasantries like entertainment or hobby spending.
- As referenced earlier, Fidelity calculated in a 2022 study that a healthy couple retiring at age sixty-five could expect to pay around $315,000 over the course of retirement to cover health and medical expenses.

I know. "Whoa, there, Barry, I was hoping to have a realistic idea of health costs, not be driven over by a cement mixer!"

The good news is, while we don't know these exact costs in advance, we know there *will* be costs. And you won't have to pay your total Medicare lifetime premiums in one day as a lump sum. Now that you have a good idea of health care costs in retirement, you can *plan* for them! That's the real point here: Planning in advance can keep you from feeling nickel-and-dimed to your wits' end. Instead, having a sizeable portion of your assets earmarked for health care can allow you the freedom to choose health care networks, coverage options, and long-term care possibilities that you like.

Product Riders

LTCI and self-funding are not the only ways to plan for the expenses of longevity. Some companies are getting creative with their products, particularly insurance companies. One way

---

[16] Merritt Whitley. A Place for Mom. May 19, 2023. "How Much Do Nursing Homes Cost? A State-By-State Guide"
https://www.aplaceformom.com/caregiver-resources/articles/nursing-homes-cost

they are retooling to meet people's needs is through optional product riders on annuities and life insurance. Elsewhere in this book, I talk about annuity basics, but here's a brief overview: Annuities are insurance contracts. You pay the insurance company a premium — either as a lump sum or as a series of payments over a set amount of time — in exchange for guaranteed income payments.

One of the advantages of an annuity is it has access to riders, which allow you to tweak your contract for a fee — usually about 0.1 percent to 1 percent of the contract value per year.[17] One annuity rider some companies offer is a long-term care rider. If you have an annuity with a long-term care rider and are not in need of long-term care, your contract behaves as any annuity contract would — nothing changes. Generally speaking, if you reach a point when you can't perform multiple functions of daily life on your own, you notify the insurance company, and if you meet the long-term care rider requirements, your additional rider benefits can be activated to help you pay for your long-term care needs. An insurance company representative will turn on those provisions of your contract. Activating LTC rider benefits is more involved than simply calling your insurance carrier. A physician has to confirm that you cannot perform the required amount of activities of daily living (ADLs).

Like LTCI, different companies and products offer different options. Some annuity long-term care riders offer coverage of two years in a nursing home situation. Others cap expenses at two times the original annuity's value. It greatly depends. Some people prefer this option because there isn't a "use-it-or-lose-it" piece; if you die without ever having needed long-term care, you still will have had the income benefit from the base contract.

---

[17] Shawn Plummer. The Annuity Expert. 2024. "Annuity Fees: What You Need To Know" https://www.annuityexpertadvice.com/types-of-annuities/annuity-fees/

Still, as with any annuities or insurance contracts, there are the usual restrictions and limitations. Withdrawing money from the contract will affect future income payments, early distributions can result in a penalty, income taxes may apply, and, because the insurance company's solvency is what guarantees your payments, it's important to do your research about the insurance company you are considering purchasing a contract from.

Understandably, a discussion on long-term care is bound to feel at least a little tedious. Yet, it is an important piece of planning for income in retirement, particularly if you want to leave a legacy.

Many families avoid addressing long-term care due to its high costs. However, it's crucial to confront this inevitability. Similar to the reluctance to discuss death, people tend to shy away from the topic of getting sick and being in a care facility because, ultimately, it leads to the same outcome, death.

As astonishing as it may sound, some individuals in their nineties haven't even discussed their estate plans with their children. Consequently, the children, now in their seventies, are left with uncertainty after their parents pass away. This lack of communication extends to health care decisions, where individuals pretend they can avoid dealing with the issue until it flies into their faces.

Failing to allocate resources in the right places can have dire financial consequences for the entire family. Let's say a husband encounters long-term needs. If funds are taken from savings before the husband subsequently passes away, consider the aftermath for his wife. Without any financial resources or a means to pay for her own long-term care, she may need to manage independently for the next twenty years with substantially fewer assets. Frankly, this situation would be challenging for her to navigate.

I consider that kind of fallout to be unloving, uncaring, and selfish. Caring people take steps to protect their loved ones. If someone comes to me and thinks they can't take care of their loved ones when a medical crisis arises because it's too expensive to prepare for the inevitable, I show them their true math. Together, we'll devise a long-term care strategy as part of their overall retirement plan. Often, the numbers turn out to work. But if they don't, we'll revise the strategy until they do. Some kind of long-term care strategy is better than none at all.

Spousal Planning

Here's one thing to keep in mind no matter how you plan to save: Many of us will be planning for more than ourselves. Look back at all the stats on health events and the likelihood of long life and long-term care. If they hold true for a single individual, then the likelihood of having a costly health or long-term care event is even higher for a married couple. You'll be planning for not just one life, but two. So, when it comes to long-term care insurance, annuities, self-funding, or whatever strategy you are looking at using, be sure you are funding longevity for the both of you.

CHAPTER 2
Taxes

Where to begin with taxes? Perhaps by acknowledging we all bear responsibility for the resources we share such as roads, bridges, and schools. Every American's patriotic duty is to pay their fair share of taxes. Many would agree with me. However, while they don't mind paying their fair share, they're not interested in paying one cent more than that!

Now, just talking about taxes probably takes your mind to April — tax season. You are probably thinking about all the forms you collect and how you file. Perhaps you are thinking about your certified public accountant or another qualified tax professional and saying to yourself, "I've already got taxes taken care of, thanks!"

However, what I see when people come into my office is that their relationship with their tax professional is purely a January through April relationship. That means they may have a tax *professional,* but not a tax *planner.*

What I mean is tax planning extends beyond filing taxes. In April, we are required to settle our accounts with the IRS to make sure we have paid up on our bill or even the score if we have overpaid. But real tax planning is about making each financial move in a way that allows you to keep the most money in your pocket and out of Uncle Sam's.

I see the way taxes affect my clients, and I have plenty of experience helping clients implement tax-efficient strategies in their retirement plans in conjunction with their tax professionals.

Our company provides assistance to clients if they find themselves navigating tax troubles with the IRS. Furthermore, we develop tax strategies for our corporate clients that often lead to significant six-figure reductions in income tax liability each year. Even our regular retirement clients can benefit greatly from lesser-known opportunities that can result in multiple six-figure savings over their lifetimes.

It is especially important to me to help my clients develop tax-efficient strategies in their retirement plans because each dollar they can keep in their pockets is a dollar we can put to work.

The government already has a plan for your taxes. And guess what? You probably won't like it. When you reach the age when you must take required minimum distributions from retirement accounts (age seventy-three for people born from 1951 to 1959, and age seventy-five for those born in the 1960s), Americans confront a challenge. You lose control over when you take income. Also, the government dictates how much income you're forced to withdraw from your IRAs, and which tax bracket you fall into.

However, you can establish control if you take action well before RMDs begin. You can implement a tax strategy. You can even manipulate your income to fit the tax brackets that work in your favor. Don't wait until the government forces your hand and takes away all your control. Be proactive and avoid becoming a victim of tax policy.

The Fed

Now, in the United States, taxes can be a rather uncertain proposition. Depending on who is in the White House and which party controls Congress, we might be tempted to assume tax rates could either decline or increase in the next four to eight years accordingly. However, there is one (large!) factor we, as a nation, must confront: the national debt.

Currently, according to USDebtClock.org, we are over $34,000,000,000,000 in debt and climbing. That's $34 *trillion* with a "T." With just $1 trillion, you could park it in the bank at a zero percent interest rate and spend more than $54 million every day for fifty years without hitting a zero balance.

Even if Congress got a handle and stopped that debt from its daily compound, divided by each taxpayer, we each would owe about $267,000. So, will that be check, cash, or Venmo?[18]

My point here isn't to give you anxiety. I'm just cautioning you that even with the rosiest of outlooks on our personal income tax rates, none of us should count on low tax rates for the long term. Instead, you and your network of professionals (tax, legal, and financial) should constantly be looking for ways to take advantage of tax-saving opportunities as they come. After all, the most ideal "luck" is when proper planning meets opportunity.

So, how can we get started?

Know Your Limits

One of the foundational pieces of tax planning is knowing and understanding your marginal tax rate. Marginal tax rate is the tax rate you pay on your highest dollar of income. In the United States, we use a progressive tax system, meaning your marginal tax rate increases as your taxable income increases. However, to be clear, not all of your income is taxed at that highest rate — only the upper portion.

A taxpayer's income is divided into tax brackets, and the brackets determine the rate applied to increments of the filer's taxable income.

For example, if your single friend tells you she is in the 22 percent tax bracket, that means her highest amount of income is taxed at 22 percent, but chunks of her income are taxed at

---

[18] usdebtclock.org. Accessed May 29, 2024.

lower rates. Using the 2024 tax bracket below, her first $11,600 of income will be taxed at 10 percent, but her next chunk of income ($11,601 to $47,150) will be taxed at 12 percent. Finally, her income, beginning at $47,151, will be taxed at 22 percent. Her tax owed for the year — before any additional taxes or credits — is the accumulation of those three amounts.

2024 Tax Brackets: Single Filers		
Tax Rate	**Taxable Income Bracket**	**Tax Owed**
10%	$0 to $11,600	10% of taxable income.
12%	$11,601 to $47,150	$1,160 plus 12% of the amount over $11,600
22%	$47,151 to $100,525	$5,426 plus 22% of the amount over $47,150
24%	$100,526 to $191,950	$17,168.50 plus 24% of the amount over $100,525
32%	$191,951 to $243,725	$39,110.50 plus 32% of the amount over $191,950
35%	$243,726 to $609,350	$55,678.50 plus 35% of the amount over $243,725
37%	$609,351 or more	$183,647.25 plus 37% of the amount over $609,350

[19]

It's important to note the difference between marginal and effective tax rates. The effective tax rate represents the

---

[19] Sabrina Parys and Tina Orem. NerdWallet. April 15, 2024. "2023 and 2024 Tax Brackets and Federal Income Tax Rates" https://www.nerdwallet.com/article/taxes/federal-income-tax-brackets

percentage of taxable income an individual pays in taxes. To calculate the effective rate, take the total dollar amount you pay in income tax and divide it by your total income. Thus, it is the average rate and is almost always a lower percentage than a marginal rate.

Why are marginal and effective rates important in retirement planning? Federal income tax is one of the biggest expenses individuals pay in their lives. In some cases, the lifetime amount can exceed lifetime mortgage payments. Although there are federal tax breaks for Americans over the age of sixty-five, many former high-income earners continue to pay income taxes. Estimating your marginal tax rate is one of the components in determining when to begin Social Security and a crucial factor regarding Roth IRA conversions. Also, a thorough analysis of current and future marginal tax rates is important in the strategic planning for required minimum distributions (RMDs) on tax-deferred retirement accounts.

Assuming a Lower Tax Rate

Retirement has always been imagined as a time when you stop working and no longer earn wages or self-employment income. In the past, Social Security benefits were not subject to taxation. Even though pensions were usually taxable, their income stream didn't fully replace a recipient's previous salary. If you needed to pull from your investment funds during retirement, keep in mind that the principal had already been taxed. In general, prior to the 1970s, your income during retirement — your cash inflow – was usually taxed at a lower rate than when you were working because you had less income and certain portions of it were not taxable.

In 1978, lawmakers created Section 401 of the Internal Revenue Code to prevent companies from using tax-advantaged profit-sharing plans to primarily benefit executives. However, businessman Ted Benna reimagined this code as the foundation of the modern 401(k). This innovation ultimately led to the decline of traditional company pension plans, while shifting both control and risk to employees. The most significant change was the shift of taxation from when employees were paid and when investment income was earned to the time of withdrawal. This tax advantage encouraged individuals to save more money in tax-deferred plans than they would have in regular savings accounts, up to the allowed limits.

In addition, in 1983, Social Security introduced new tax brackets to address the problem of decreasing reserves. This resulted in both the potential for Social Security to become taxable and a significant shift in retirement planning strategy. Within a five-year period, the retirement planning landscape changed for decades going forward, possibly forever.

A big selling point for qualified retirement accounts (401(k)s, 403(b)s, IRAs, etc.) is the theory that people will pay less in tax during their retirement years than during their working years when they're putting that money away. The idea is that you're allowed to "defer" paying the tax on that income until your marginal tax rate drops in retirement. Hence, you pay less in tax on that income.

But what if it doesn't pan out that way? For some retirees, their marginal tax rate will stay the same in retirement or even increase. If you have a healthy balance in your qualified retirement account, combining its RMDs or even a Roth conversion with Social Security can result in what is called the "tax torpedo." This tax increase occurs when a larger percent of your Social Security becomes taxable, and that same income increase consequently bumps a taxpayer up to a higher marginal rate.

401(k)s/IRAs/Roth IRAs

One sometimes-unexpected piece of tax planning in retirement concerns the 401(k) or IRA. Most of us have one of these accounts or an equivalent. We pay in throughout our working lives, dutifully socking away a portion of our earnings in these tax-deferred accounts. There's the rub: tax-*deferred*, not tax-

free. Very rarely is anything free of taxation when you get down to it. Using 401(k)s and IRAs in retirement is no different. The taxes the government deferred when you were in your working years are now coming due, and you will pay taxes on that income at whatever your current tax rate is.

Just to ensure Uncle Sam gets his due, the government also has an RMD rule. Beginning at age seventy-three (or seventy-five if you were born in 1960 or after), you are required to withdraw a certain minimum amount every year from your 401(k) or IRA, or else you will face a tax penalty on any RMD monies you should have withdrawn but didn't — and that's on top of income tax. The SECURE Act 2.0 reduced the penalty to 25 percent (from 50 percent). Timely corrections also can further reduce the penalty to 10 percent.[20]

Of course, there is also the Roth account. You can think of the difference between a Roth and a traditional retirement account as the difference between taxing the seed and taxing the harvest. Because Roths get funded with post-tax dollars, there aren't tax penalties for early withdrawals of the principal, nor are there taxes on the growth after you reach age fifty-nine-and-one-half. Perhaps best of all, there are no RMDs. Of course, you must own a Roth account for a minimum of five years before you are able to take advantage of all its features.

This is one more area where it pays to be aware of your marginal tax rate. Some people may opt to put any excess RMDs from their traditional retirement accounts into stocks or insurance. Others may find it advantageous to "convert" their traditional retirement account funds to Roth account funds in a year during which they are in a lower tax bracket.

---

[20] Jim Probasco. Investopedia. October 20, 2023. "SECURE 2.0 Act of 2022: Overview, Rules, Limits." https://www.investopedia.com/secure-2-0-definition-5225115

Roth IRA Conversions

A Roth conversion simply means converting (or withdrawing) monies from your traditional, tax-deferred retirement accounts and moving them to a Roth account. Once inside the Roth, any growth on these funds will accumulate completely tax-free, and tax will not be owed when the Roth funds are withdrawn, assuming the conditions noted above. This is an exciting opportunity for accumulation! However, a thoughtful strategy is beneficial in the conversion process. Since dollars were placed into the traditional account pre-tax and the growth is taxable in these accounts, tax is owed on *all* the money converted to the Roth. Converting an employer plan account to a Roth IRA is a taxable event. Increased taxable income from the Roth IRA conversion may have several consequences, including (but not limited to) a need for additional tax withholding or estimated tax payments, the loss of certain tax deductions and credits, higher taxes on Social Security benefits, and higher Medicare premiums.

Points to consider regarding a conversion:

How are you going to pay the tax? Again, any time you withdraw funds from a 401(k) or traditional IRA, tax is owed on 100 percent of that money, whether the distribution was a basic withdrawal, an RMD, or a Roth conversion. In addition to the income tax, if the account owner is younger than fifty-nine-and-one-half, it is most likely a 10 percent tax penalty will be assessed. So, if you're under fifty-nine-and-one-half and have a year when your income is lower – reducing your marginal tax rate – you need to weigh the amount of the tax penalty against the decrease in ordinary income tax.

As a tricky sidenote, if you are under fifty-nine-and-one-half and you have tax withheld from your conversion and sent directly to the government, you will not escape the 10 percent penalty.

Did you compare your current tax rate to your estimated future rate? As mentioned above, a good time to consider a Roth is in a year when your taxable income — and thus your marginal tax rate — is lower than normal or lower than expected in the future. A popular conversion strategy is to transfer funds during a period referred to as "the trough years." That is the period after you've retired but before you begin receiving Social Security or are required to begin RMDs. It is easier to manage the tax on the conversion during these years as you have more control over the sources and the amounts of your income.

What is your Roth withdrawal strategy? There are four considerations here.
- Can you leave converted money in the Roth for at least five years? You must leave your converted money in the Roth for at least five years for the withdrawals to be tax-free. That five-year countdown begins on January 1 of the year you made the conversion, even if your conversion date was December 31. This five-year countdown applies in each year you make a conversion.
- Even if you hold the Roth funds for five years, you will still face penalties for withdrawals if you're under fifty-nine-and-one-half.[21]
- The longer you leave funds inside the Roth after the conversion, the more time it can grow and potentially recoup the tax levied on your traditional account's withdrawals. Remember, this money is now growing tax-free. A long growth period may be able to outweigh a loss in your balance due to income tax withholdings at conversion time. Also, an error in estimates of future tax rate margins (i.e., your future rates turned out to be less than the conversion year)

---

[21] Kailey Hagen. The Motley Fool. November 16, 2022. "4 Things to Know If You're Considering a Roth IRA Conversion This Year"
https://www.fool.com/retirement/2022/11/16/4-things-to-know-if-youre-considering-a-roth-ira-c/

can be made up by holding funds in your Roth for many years.[22]
- Planning to use your Roth as a legacy planning tool? There are various rules and options depending on the type of heir, but in most cases the Roth is given additional time to grow tax-free.

Does that make your head spin? Understandable. That's why it's so important to work with a financial professional and tax planner who can help you execute these sorts of tax-efficient strategies and help you understand what you are doing and why.

---

[22] Tim Steffen. Baird Private Wealth Management. October 16, 2023. "The Three Tests Before a Roth Conversion" https://www.bairdwealth.com/insights/wealth-management-perspectives/2023/09/the-three-tests-before-a-roth-conversion/

CHAPTER 3
Market Volatility

Up and down. Roller coaster. Merry-go-round. Bulls and bears. Peak-to-trough.

Sound familiar? This is the language we use to talk about the stock market. With volatility and spikes, even our language is jarring, bracing, and vivid.

Still, financial strategies tend to revolve around market-based products, and for good reasons. For one thing, there is no other financial class that packs the same potential for growth, pound for pound, as stock-based products. Because of growth potential, inflation challenges, and new opportunities, it may be unwise to avoid the market entirely.

However, along with the potential for growth is the potential for loss. At the time this book was written, many of the people I've seen in my office came in feeling uneasy because of the economic fallout of the COVID-19 outbreak of 2020, followed by the economic downturn and the inflation spike that happened in 2022.

So, how do we balance these factors? How do we try to satisfy both the need for protection and the need for growth?

For one thing, it is important to recognize the value of diversity. Now, I'm not just talking about the diversity of assets among different kinds of stocks, or even different kinds of stocks and bonds. That's only one kind of diversity. Stocks and bonds, though different, are both still important market-based products. Even within a diverse portfolio, most market-based products tend to rise or fall as a whole, just like an incoming tide. Therefore, a portfolio diverse in only market-sourced products won't automatically preserve your assets during times when the market declines.

In addition to the sort of "horizontal diversity" you have by purchasing a variety of stocks and bonds from different companies, I also suggest you think about "vertical diversity," or diversity among asset classes. This means having different product types, including securities products, bank products, and insurance products — with varying levels of growth potential, liquidity, and protection — all in accordance with your unique situation, goals, and needs.

We often see clients who tell us how conservative they are with their investments. And, when we put them through our process to determine their comfortability with various levels of risk, they will indeed score out quite conservatively. But when we move on to analyze potential volatility that could arise in their portfolios, we'll find that their investments are far from conservative. They're embracing (often unknowingly) much more risk than they said they were comfortable taking.

We use statistical analysis that lists risk scores figuratively measured in miles per hour. It's not unusual to have a person state a risk preference of 35 mph, only to discover the risk they currently have in their existing investments may be zooming along at 65 mph.

Everyone knows that if you drive a car at 1 mph and have a wreck, usually nothing terrible happens. But if you drive a car at 90 mph and have a wreck, the impact could kill everybody involved and destroy the car. That's why we explain risk in terms of miles per hour. Through the use of those speed ratings, we can often build effective portfolio models that can reduce risk by 25 to 40 percent. Those models often meet clients' objectives and keep them from assuming unwarranted investment peril.

The Color of Money

When you're looking at the overall diversity of your portfolio, part of the equation is knowing which products fit in what category: what has liquidity, what has protection, and what has growth potential.

Before we dive in, keep in mind these aren't absolutes. You might think of liquidity, growth, and protection as primary colors. While some products will look pretty much yellow, red, or blue, others will have a mix of characteristics, making them more green, orange, or purple.

Growth

I like to think of the growth category as red. It's powerful, it's somewhat volatile, and it's also the category where we have the greatest opportunities for growth and loss. Often, products in the growth category will have a good deal of liquidity but very little protection. These are our market-based products and strategies, and we think of them mostly in shades of red and orange to designate their growth and liquidity. This is usually a good place to be when you're young — think fast cars and flashy leather jackets — but its allure often wanes as you move closer to retirement. Examples of "red" products include:
- Stocks
- Equities
- Exchange-traded funds
- Mutual funds
- Corporate bonds
- Real estate investment trusts
- Speculations
- Alternative investments

Liquidity

Yellow is my liquid category color. I typically recommend having at least enough yellow money to cover six months' to a year's worth of expenses in case of emergency. Yellow assets don't need a lot of growth potential; they just need to be readily available when we need them. The "yellow" category includes assets like:
- Cash
- Money market accounts

Protection

The color of protection, to me, is blue, which can incorporate products such as annuities. Tranquil, peaceful, sure — even if it lacks a certain amount of flash. This is the direction I like to see people generally move toward as they're nearing retirement. The red, flashy look of stock market returns and the risk of possible overnight losses are less attractive as we near retirement and look for more consistency and reliability. While this category doesn't come with a lot of liquidity, the products here are backed by an insurance company, a bank, or a government entity. "Blue" products include things such as:
- Certificates of deposit (backed by banks)
- Government-based bonds (backed by the U.S. government)
- Life insurance (backed by insurance companies)
- Annuities (backed by insurance companies)

I firmly believe in the incredible opportunities presented by investing in America's capital markets. Throughout our lives, these markets have proven profitable for those who possess the know-how to navigate them. And you know what? That truth isn't going to be rewritten anytime soon.

Unfortunately, there's so much that people don't know about the markets. You could fill an entire book examining the things people are unaware of. Even more shocking is that a significant portion of what people think they know isn't necessarily accurate.

So, it's clear that our issue doesn't lie with the markets themselves. The real problem is the lack of understanding among consumers about how the markets truly work and how they can safeguard themselves against potential downturns while still seizing the upside potential. It's time for everyone to break free from misconceptions and unleash the true power of the market.

401(k)s

I want to take a second to specifically address a product many retirees will be using to build their retirement income: the 401(k) and other retirement accounts. Any of these retirement accounts (IRAs, 401(k)s, 403(b)s, etc.) are basically "tax wrappers." What do I mean by that? Well, depending on your plan provider, a 401(k) could include target-date funds, passively managed products, stocks, bonds, mutual funds, or even variable, fixed, and fixed index annuities, all collected in one place and governed by rules (a.k.a. the "tax wrapper"). These rules govern how much money you can put inside, what ways you can put it in, when you will pay taxes on it, and when you can take the money out. Inside the 401(k), each of the products inside the "tax wrapper" might have its own fees or commissions, in addition to the management fee you pay on the 401(k) itself.

Now, fees can be troublesome. You can't get something for nothing, and fees are how many financial companies and professionals make a living. Yet, it's important to recognize even a fee with a fraction of a percentage point is money out of your pocket — money that represents not just the one-time fee of today but also an opportunity cost. For example, consider how a $100,000 IRA that earns 6 percent over a twenty-five-year period without investment fees would earn $430,000. But if just a 0.5 percent fee was factored into that investment, the

IRA would be worth $379,000 in twenty-five years — a $50,500 decrease. For someone close to retirement, how much do you think fees may have cost over their lifetime?

Even for those close to retirement, it's important to look at management fees and assess if you think you're getting what you pay for. Over the course of ten years, those costs can add up, and you may have decades ahead of you in which you will need to rely on your assets.

Dollar-Cost Averaging

With 401(k)s and other market-based retirement products, dollar-cost averaging is a concept that can work in your favor when you are investing for the long term. When the market is trending up, if you are consistently paying in money, month over month, great; your investments can grow, and you are adding to your assets. When the market takes a dip, no problem; your dollars buy more shares at a lower price. At some point, we hope the market will rebound, in which case your shares can grow and possibly be more valuable than they were before. This concept is what we call "dollar-cost averaging." While it can't ensure a profit or guarantee against losses, it's a time-tested strategy for investing in a volatile market.

However, when you are in retirement, this strategy may work against you. You may have heard of "reverse" dollar-cost averaging. Before, when the market lost ground, you were "bargain-shopping"; your dollars purchased more assets at a reduced price. When you are in retirement, you are no longer the purchaser; you are selling. So, in a down market, you have to sell more assets to make the same amount of money as what you made in a favorable market.

I've had lots of people step into my office to talk to me about this, emphasizing how their advisor says, "the market always bounces back, and I have to just hold on for the long term."

There's some basis for this thinking; thus far, the market has always rebounded to higher heights than before. But this is no guarantee, and the prospect of potentially higher returns in five years may not be very helpful in retirement if you are relying on the income from those returns to pay this month's electric bill, for example.

When it comes to managing your finances, one of the first things we need to establish is how much of your portfolio should be exposed to the markets and how much should be protected. Think of it like designing the architecture of your retirement house. We want to make sure that the money you want to keep safe is well protected in the basement so that even when economic storms hit, it remains untouched.

Now, for the money you're willing to invest subject to market volatility, we follow a disciplined approach. We speak of red and green lights to indicate the right time to invest or step aside. We're not concerned with what the TV pundits say. Instead, we focus on market trends. When the market is in demand, that's a green light, and you want to be part of it. It means that as more people invest, the value of your investments will rise. However, when the market goes into supply, it's a red light, and we take a step back. As money starts to leave the market, it weakens the foundation of your investments, and you don't want to be caught off guard.

It's a simple process of identifying whether the market is in supply or demand. When it's in supply, we exit the market; when it's in demand, we jump in.

When the markets are in demand, and you should be invested, the question is: where? There are eleven sectors in the S&P 500, each having their own distinct supply and demand. Our algorithms rank those sectors from top to bottom based on demand. This allows us to keep our investments concentrated in the sectors that are in demand while avoiding those sectors that are in supply.

Some may advise you to just invest in the S&P 500 and call it a day. When you do that, however, you are owning the best and the worst sectors — those in greatest demand and those in over-supply. We believe in carefully choosing the most in-demand sectors because they offer the most potential.

Is There a "Perfect" Product?

To bring us back around to the discussion of protection, growth, and liquidity, the ideal product would be a "ten" in all three categories, right? Completely guaranteed, doubling in size every few years, and accessible whenever you want. Does such a product exist? Absolutely not.

Instead of running in circles looking for that perfect product, the silver bullet, the unicorn of financial strategies, it's more important to circle back to the concept of a balanced, asset-diverse portfolio.

This is why it could be prudent to work with a knowledgeable financial professional who knows what various financial products can do and how to use them in your personal retirement strategy.*

---

* Investing involves risk, including the potential loss of principal. No investment strategy can guarantee a profit or protect against loss in periods of declining values. Any references to protection benefits or guaranteed/lifetime income streams refer only to fixed insurance products, not securities or investment products. Insurance and annuity product guarantees are backed by the financial strength and claims-paying ability of the issuing insurance company.

CHAPTER 4

Retirement Income

Retirement. For many of us, it's what we've saved for and dreamed of, pinning our hopes to a magical someday. Is that someday full of traveling? Is it filled with grandkids? Gardening? Maybe your fondest dream is simply never having to work again, never having to clock in or be accountable to someone else.

Your ability to do these things all hinges on *income*. Without the money to support these dreams, even a basic level of work-free lifestyle is unsustainable. That's why planning for your income in retirement is so foundational. But where do we begin?

It's easy to feel overwhelmed by this question. Some may feel the urge to amass a large lump sum and then try to put it all in one product — insurance, investments, liquid assets — to provide all the growth, liquidity, and income they need. Instead, I think you need a more balanced approach. After all, retirement planning isn't magic. As I mention elsewhere, there is no single product that can be all things to all people (or even all things to one person). No approach works unilaterally for everyone. That's why it's important to talk to a financial professional who can help you lay down the basics and take you step-by-step through the process. Not only will you have the assurance you have addressed the areas you need to, but you will also have an ally who can help you break down the process and help keep you from feeling overwhelmed.

Sources of Income

Thinking of all the pieces of your retirement expenses might be intimidating. But, like cleaning out a junk drawer or revisiting that garage remodel, once you have laid everything out, you can begin to sort things into categories.

Once you have a good overall picture of where your expenses will lie, you can start stacking up the resources to cover them.

Social Security

Social Security is a guaranteed, inflation-adjusted federal insurance program that plays a significant part in most of our retirement plans. From delaying until you've reached full retirement age or beyond to examining spousal benefits, as I discuss elsewhere in this book, there is plenty you can do to try to make the most of this monthly benefit. As with all your retirement income sources, it's important to consider ways to make this resource stretch to provide the most bang and buck for your situation.

Pension

Another generally reliable source of retirement income for you might be a pension, if you are one of the lucky people who still has one.

If you don't have a pension, go ahead and skim on to the next section. If you do have a pension, keep on reading.

Because your pension can be such a central piece of your retirement income plan, you will want to put some thought into answering basic questions about it.

How well is your pension funded? Since the heyday of the pension plan, companies and governments have neglected to fund their pension obligations, causing a persistent problem with this otherwise reliable asset.

Consider the factors at play, though. Pensions had been underfunded and gained a boost from strong market performance, most recently in 2021.[23] What happens to the solvency of those pension funds if the market declines?

It can be worthwhile to keep tabs on your pension's health and know what your options are for withdrawing from it. Typically, you have one chance at electing the distribution option at your retirement with no recourse to change at a later date, so you will want to look at all options before making a final decision. If you have already retired and made those decisions, this may be a foregone conclusion. If not, it pays to know what you can expect and what decisions you can make, such as taking spousal options to cover your spouse if they outlive you.

Also, some companies are incentivizing lump-sum payouts of pensions to reduce the companies' payment liabilities. If that's the case with your employer, talk to your financial professional to see if it might be prudent to do something like that or if it might be better to stick with lifetime payments or other options.

Your 401(k) and IRA

One "modern way" to save for retirement is in a 401(k) or IRA (or their nonprofit or governmental equivalents). These tax-advantaged accounts are, in my opinion, a poor substitute for pensions, but one of the biggest disservices we do to ourselves is not taking full advantage of them in the first place. While the average 401(k) balance for Americans between the ages of forty and forty-nine is $105,500, the median account balance is

---

[23] The Pew Charitable Trusts. November 8, 2023. "Public Retirement Systems Need Sustainable Policies to Navigate Volatile Financial Markets" https://www.pewtrusts.org/en/research-and-analysis/issue-briefs/2023/11/public-retirement-systems-need-sustainable-policies-to-navigate-volatile-financial-markets

much lower. The median, which separates half of accounts with higher balances and half with lower balances, is just $34,100.[24]

Also, if you have changed jobs over the years, do the work of tracking down any benefits from your past employers. You might have an IRA here or a 401(k) there; keep track of those so you can pull them together and look at those assets when you're ready to look at establishing sources of retirement income.

Do You Have ...

- Life insurance?
- Annuities?
- Long-term care insurance?
- Any passive income sources?
- Stock and bond portfolios?
- Liquid assets? (What's in your bank account?)
- Alternative investments?
- Rental properties?

If you are going through the work of sitting with a financial professional, it's important to look at your full retirement income picture and pull together *all* your assets, no matter how big or small. From the free insurance policy offered at your bank to the sizable investment in your brother-in-law's modestly successful furniture store, you want to have a good idea of where your money is.

One of our clients worked for a publicly traded company in Springfield. He made around $45,000 annually. He and his wife were perfectly content with their lives. They knew they owned some stock in that company, but only had a vague idea of how much. They had these stock certificates hidden away in their dining room cupboard drawer, just collecting dust.

---

[24] Cheyenne DeVon. CNBC. July 13, 2023. "Here's how much Americans in their 40s have in their 401(k)s"
https://www.cnbc.com/2023/07/13/fidelity-how-much-americans-in-their-40s-have-in-their-401ks.html

We began digging everything up and figured out the stock's value. The final tally revealed they had around $2.5 million. Essentially, they hit the jackpot. They could retire and do virtually anything they wanted.

Yet a problem surfaced. Most of their savings were tied up in one stock. The stock had been shooting up for some time, but what would happen if it crashed? People sometimes do not realize such a fallout could happen to them — just like those folks at Enron. Enron's stock tumbled from a high of $90 per share in mid-2000 to less than $.12 (that's 12 cents!) roughly a year later when its stock crashed.[25] Sometimes, people can grow so euphoric over market gains that they don't consider what it would mean if their favorite investment and largest holding stumbles. It could ruin their retirement.

With clients astounded by sudden fortune, I find it necessary to caution them to trim their position and take some of the profits from their unexpected largess. In this case, they agreed. We started selling that stock, and guess what? It kept going up. We shook our heads with a bit of chagrin as the stock soared higher and higher. Yet we never considered it a bad strategy. Instead of the additional opportunity we missed, we focused on the risks we avoided. So, in this case, as the stock continued to climb, we used a special strategy that effectively insured their stock against going down in value. We paid for insurance that protected them if the stock ever declined appreciably.

Retirement Income Needs

How much income will you need in retirement? How do you determine that? A lot of people work toward a random number, thinking, "If I can just have a million dollars, I'll be comfortable in retirement!" Don't get me wrong; it is possible to save up a lot of money and then retire in the hopes you can keep your monthly expenses lower than some set estimation. But I think

---

[25] Peter Bondarenko. Brittanica. August 11, 2023. "Enron scandal" https://www.britannica.com/event/Enron-scandal

this carries a general risk of running out of money. Instead, I work with my clients to find out what their current and projected income needs are and then work from there to see how we might cover any gaps between what they have and what they want.

Goals and Dreams

I like to start with your pie in the sky. Do you find yourself planning for your vacations more thoroughly than you do your retirement? Maybe it's because planning a vacation is less stressful: Having a week at the beach go awry is, well, a walk on the beach compared to running out of money in retirement. Whatever the case, perhaps it would be better if you thought of your retirement as a vacation in and of itself — no clocking in, no boss, no overtime. If you felt unlimited by financial strain, what would you do?

Would an endless vacation for you mean Paris and Rome? Would it mean mentoring at children's clubs or serving at the local soup kitchen? Or maybe it would mean deepening your ties to those immediately around you — neighbors, friends, and family. Perhaps it would mean more time to take part in the hobbies and activities you love. Have you been considering a second (or even third) act as a small-business owner, turning a hobby or passion into a revenue source?

This is your time to daydream and answer the question: If you could do anything, what would you do?

After that, it's a matter of putting a dollar amount on it. What are the costs of round-the-world travel? One couple I know said their highest priority in retirement was being able to take each of their grandchildren on a cross-country vacation every year. That's a pretty specific goal — one that is reasonably easy to nail down a budget for.

As people approach retirement, we ask them questions about their goals and dreams. Yet it is incredible how many people lack retirement ambition. Our culture and daily life in America tend to crush people's dreams, and that trains them not to dream. Even when people do dream of retirement, they often don't have any dreams about what they will do during retirement.

That's where our process comes in. We help people dream about retiring. We use an imaginative exercise where we figuratively hire the renowned painter Norman Rockwell to create a painting of their retirement. They have the responsibility to tell Norman everything they want in the painting. We ask them to speak separately, the husband and wife.

Grandchildren are usually mentioned, and sometimes pets. Hobbies and leisurely activities come up often. Mr. Rockwell's canvas could include a cozy cabin by a lake, a game of golf on a celebrated course, or an exotic vacation with sandy beaches or mountain views. Maybe a rod is bent on some fishing lake, or a dinner table features a delicious feast.

We design our process to encourage people to dream. It's okay to say out loud what you want in retirement; if it's within our power to do so, we'll help you achieve it. Though many participants still don't leave with bigger goals, we've encouraged them to think about what they want to do in retirement. It's crucial to know not only what you're retiring from but what you're retiring to.

Not thinking adequately about your retirement dreams and what you want to do in retirement is why many people eventually return to work. Personally, I may never quit working myself because I'd need something better and more satisfying to retire to than what I'm doing now, and I love what I am doing now! But the possibilities are worth exploring and certainly worth the time to open your mind as you enter this new season of your life.

Current Budget

Compiling a current expense report is one of the trickiest pieces of retirement preparation. Many people assume the expenses of their lives in retirement will be lower. After all, there will be no drive to work, no need for a formal wardrobe, and — perhaps most impactful of all — no more saving for retirement!

Yet, we often underestimate our daily spending habits. That's why I typically ask my clients to bring in their bank statements for the past year — they are reflective of your *actual* spending, not just what you think you're spending.

Imagine you're sitting on your front porch, watching the world go by. No worries, no work. Just pure relaxation. Now think about this: How much money would you need to deposit into your bank account every month to cover all your bills and meet your needs if sitting on the porch is all you do?

You might say, "I don't want to just sit on the porch!" But that's missing the point of this exercise. It's not about sitting on the porch; it's about knowing how much it takes to fund your lifestyle in retirement.

It's fascinating to me how some people struggle with this. Many people don't live on a budget or even know if they can achieve financial security. One way to answer this question is to look at how much money you're actually earning right now and whether you are spending it all or have some left at the end of the month. This is a way we can work backward to figure out your "sitting on the porch" number.

I can't count the number of times I have sat with a couple, asked them about their spending, and heard them throw out a number that seemed incredibly low. When I ask them where the number came from, they usually say they estimated based on their total bills. Yet, our spending is so much more than our mortgage, utilities, cable, phone, car, grocery, or credit card bills.

"What about clothes?" I ask, "Or dining out? What about gifts and coffees and last-minute birthday cards?" That's when the lights come on.

This is why I suggest collecting a year's worth of information. There is usually no such thing as a one-time purchase. Did you buy new furniture? Even if that is a rarity, do you think that will be the last time you *ever* buy furniture?

A woman walked into my office one day, sat down and requested I create an income plan that allowed her $72,000 to live on annually, or $6,000 a month. She also wanted $5,000 a month for all her travel adventures. Now, $5,000 a month is quite a generous travel budget. But here's the exciting part — we did the math and discovered that she had saved enough money to cover half that travel budget. That's $30,000 a year to travel! That'll buy some nice experiences. She was thrilled to hear this news, and who could blame her?

I also remember another client, a distinguished nurse, first visiting me. After totaling her assets, she couldn't contain her excitement after learning the amount she had saved could sustain an acceptable level of income in retirement.

Such reactions are not surprising. Many people have no idea how to estimate their retirement income, how long their money will last, or if it will be enough. Consequently, they enter retirement in a state of fear and uncertainty. But here's the thing — we don't want you to hunker down in retirement; we want you to blossom into it.

We want you to enjoy your retirement without any worries, understanding where your financial boundaries lie. The problem is that most people don't know how to set those boundaries. That's where we come in. We show them precisely where those boundaries are so they can spend money confidently in retirement. Suddenly, their entire outlook brightens.

Another hefty expense is spending on the kids. Many of the couples I work with are quick to help their adult children, whether it's something like letting them live in the basement, paying for college, babysitting, paying an occasional bill, or contributing to a grandchild's college fund. Research concluded that 54 percent of those in the Gen Z and millennial age groups lean on parents for financial support. Among those, 23 percent are heavily supported by parents.[26]

---

[26] Experian. June 27, 2023. "Most Gen Zers and millennials still rely on parents for financial support and feel ashamed asking for help"

My clients sometimes protest that what they do for their grown children can stop in retirement. They don't *need* to help. But I get it. Parents like to feel needed. And, while you never want to neglect saving for retirement in favor of taking on financial risks (like your child's student debt), the parents who help their adult children do so in part because it helps them feel fulfilled.

When it comes down to expenses, including (and especially) spending on your family, don't make your initial calculations based on what you *could* whittle your budget down to if you *had* to. Instead, start from where you are. Who wants to live off a bare-bones bank account in retirement?

Other Expenses

Once you have nailed down your current budget and your dreams or goals for retirement, there are a few other outstanding pieces to think about — some expenses many people don't take the time to consider before making and executing a plan. But I'm assuming you want to get it right, so let's take a look.

Housing

Do you know where you want to live in retirement? This makes up a substantial piece of your income puzzle — since the typical American household owns a home, and it's generally their largest asset.

Some people prefer to live right where they are for as long as they can. Others have been waiting for retirement to pull the trigger on an ambitious move, like purchasing a new house, or even downsizing. Whatever your plans and whatever your reasons, there are quite a few things to consider.

---

https://www.experianplc.com/newsroom/press-releases/2023/most-gen-zers-and-millennials-still-rely-on-parents-for-financial-support-and-feel-ashamed-asking-for-help

Mortgage

Do you still have a mortgage? What may have been a nice tax boon in your working years could turn into a financial burden in your retirement. After all, when you are on a limited income, a mortgage is just one more bill sapping your financial strength. It is something to put some thought into, whether you plan to age in place or are considering moving to your dream home, buying a house out of state, or living in a retirement community.

Upkeep and Taxes

A house without a mortgage still requires annual taxes. While it's tempting to think of this as a once-a-year expense, when you have limited earning potential, your annual tax bill might be something into which you should put a little more forethought.

The costs of homeownership aren't just monetary. When you find yourself dealing with more house than you need, it can drain your time and energy. From keeping clutter at bay to keeping the lawn mower running, upkeep can be extensive and expensive. For some, that's a challenge they heartily accept and can comfortably take on. For others, the idea of yard work or cleaning an area larger than they need feels foolish.

For instance, Peggy discovered after her knee replacement that most of her house was inaccessible to her when she was laid up.

"It felt ridiculous to pay someone else to dust and vacuum a house I was only living in 40 percent of!"

Practicality and Adaptability

Erik and Marla are looking to retire within the next two decades. They just sold their old three-bedroom ranch-style house. Their twins are in high school, and the couple has wanted to "upgrade" for years. Now, they live in a gorgeous 1940s three-story house with all the kitchen space they ever wanted, five sprawling bedrooms, and a library and media room for themselves and their children. Within months of moving in, the couple realized a house perfect for their active teens would no longer be perfect for them in five to fifteen years.

"We are paying the mortgage for this house, but we've started saving for the next one," said Marla, "because who wants to climb two flights of stairs to their bedroom when they're seventy-eight?"

Others I know have encountered a similar situation in their personal lives. After a health crisis, one couple found the luxurious tub for two they toiled to install had become a specter of a bad slip and a potential safety risk. It's important to think through what your physical reality could be. I always emphasize to my clients that they should plan for whatever their long-term future might hold, but it's amazing how many people don't give it much thought.

Contracts and Regulations

If you are looking into a cross-country move, be aware of new tax tables or local ordinances in the area where you are looking to move. After all, you don't want to experience sticker-shock when you are looking at downsizing or reducing your bills in retirement.

Along the same lines, if you are moving into a retirement community, be sure to look at the fine print. What happens if you must move into a different situation for long-term care? Will you be penalized? Will you be responsible for replacing your slot in the community? What are all the fees, and what do they cover?

Inflation

As I write this in 2024, America has experienced a wave of inflation following a lengthy period of low inflation. Inflation zoomed to 9.1 percent in June 2022, its highest mark since

November 1981.[27] By the end of 2023, the inflation rate decreased to 3.1 percent.[28]

Core inflation is yet another measurement that excludes goods with prices that tend to be more volatile, such as food and energy costs. Core inflation for a twelve-month period ending in November 2023 was 4.0 percent. It so happened that energy prices decreased 5.4 percent over that timeframe.[29]

However, inflation isn't a one-time bump; it has a cumulative effect. Again, that can impact the price of groceries more than other goods. Even with relatively low inflation over the past few decades, an item you bought in 1997 for $2 will cost about $3.89 today.[30] Want to go to a show? A $20 ticket in 1997 would cost $45.12 in 2024.[31]

What if we hit a stretch in retirement like the late seventies and early eighties, when annual inflation rates of 10 percent became the norm? It may be wise to consider some extra padding in your retirement income plan to account for any potential increase in inflation in the future.

Shrinkflation

Another important yet often overlooked factor to consider is called "shrinkflation." Essentially a form of hidden inflation,

---

[27] Trading Economics. 2024. "United States Inflation Rate" https://tradingeconomics.com/united-states/inflation-cpi
[28] Statista. April 15, 2024. "Monthly 12-month inflation rate in the United States from March 2020 to March 2024" https://www.statista.com/statistics/273418/unadjusted-monthly-inflation-rate-in-the-us
[29] U.S. Inflation Calculator. 2024. "United States Core Inflation Rates (1957-2024)" https://www.usinflationcalculator.com/inflation/united-states-core-inflation-rates/
[30] in2013dollars.com. 2024. "$2 in 1997 is worth $3.89 today" https://www.in2013dollars.com/us/inflation/1997?amount=2
[31] in2013dollars.com. 2024. "Admission to movies, theaters, and concerts priced at $20 in 1997 ->$45.12 in 2024" https://www.in2013dollars.com/Admission-to-movies,-theaters,-and-concerts/price-inflation

shrinkflation signifies a reduction in packaging while retaining a similar price as before.

For example, as you walk down a grocery store aisle, you spot your favorite pickles. The jar still costs the same — roughly $5 — and you add it to your cart. Then you get home, and the container seems different after digging out a few crispy dills. You examine the jar and discover it contains fewer ounces than previous jars you purchased. However, you paid roughly the same price for your pickles.

Now, move over to the aisle featuring salty snacks. You might notice a sale on a certain brand of chips, though you must buy three or four bags to receive a discount promoted by the store. You decide to purchase that many bags to capitalize on the lower price. When you get home, you notice the packaging is smaller than you anticipated. The deal you accepted may not have been as thrifty as you perceived.

Shrinkflation can be a way for companies to quietly boost, or retain, profit margins without having to change much else — essentially, they are simply charging the same price for less product. Companies do this because customers are more likely to spot price increases than size reductions. However, research has also shown that these shrinkflation tactics can backfire into negative consumer perceptions of their brands once they come to light. Who wants to pay the same for less, especially when they have already grown accustomed to getting more for their money's worth?[32]

Aging

Also, in the expense category, think about longevity. We all hope to age gracefully. However, it's important to face the prospect of aging with a sense of realism.

---

[32] Daniel Liberto. Investopedia. November 16, 2023. "Shrinkflation: What It Is, Reasons for It, How to Spot It"
https://www.investopedia.com/terms/s/shrinkflation.asp

For many families, the elephant in the room is long-term care. No one wants to admit they will likely need it, but estimates indicate almost 70 percent of us will.[33] Aging is a significant piece of retirement income planning because you'll want to figure out how to set aside money for your care, either at home or away from it. The more comfortable you get with discussing your wishes and plans with your loved ones, the easier planning for the financial side of it can be.

I denote health care and potential long-term care costs in more detail elsewhere in this book, but suffice it to say nursing home care tends to be very expensive and typically isn't something you get to choose when you need it.

It isn't just the costs of long-term care that pose a concern in living longer. It's also about covering the possible costs of everything else associated with living longer. For instance, if Henry retires from his job as a biochemical engineer at age sixty-five, perhaps he plans to have a very decent income for twenty years until he turns eighty-five. But what if he lives until he's ninety-five? That's a whole third — ten years — more of personal income he will need.

Putting It All Together

Whew! So, you have pulled together what you have, and you have a pretty good idea of where you want to be. Now, you and your financial professional can go about the work of arranging what assets you *have* to cover what you *need* — and how you might try to cover any gaps.

Like the proverbial man in the Bible who built his house on a rock, I like to help my clients figure out how to cover their day-to-day living expenses — their needs — with insurance and other guaranteed income sources like pensions and Social Security.

---

[33] Moll Law Group. 2024. "The Cost of Long-Term Care" https://www.molllawgroup.com/the-cost-of-long-term-care.html

Again, you should keep in mind there isn't one single financial vehicle, asset, or source to fill all your needs, and that's okay. One of the challenges of planning for your income in retirement concerns figuring out what products and strategies to use. You can release some of that stress when you accept the fact you will probably need a diverse portfolio — potentially with bonds, stocks, insurance, and other income sources — not just one massive money pile.

One way to help shore up your income gaps is by working with your financial professional and a qualified tax advisor to help mitigate your tax exposure. If you have a 401(k) or IRA, a tax advisor in your corner may be able to help you figure out how and when to take distributions from your account in a way that doesn't push you into a higher tax bracket. Or you might learn of ways to use tax-advantaged bonds more effectively. Effective tax planning isn't necessarily about "adding" to your income. Especially regarding retirement, it's less about what you make than it is about what you keep. Paying a lower tax bill keeps more money in your pocket, which is where you want it when it comes to retirement income.

Now, you can look at ways to cover your remaining retirement goals. Are there products like long-term care insurance specific to a certain kind of expense you anticipate? Is there a particular asset you want to use for your "play" money — money for trips and gifts for the grandkids? Is there any way you can portion off money for those charitable legacy plans?

Once you have analyzed your income wants, needs, and the assets necessary to realistically cover them, you may have a gap. The masterstroke of a competent financial professional will be to help you figure out how you will cover that gap. Will you need to cut out a round of golf a week? Maybe skip the new car? Or will you need to take more substantial action?

One way to cover an income gap is to consider working longer or even part-time before retirement and even after that magical calendar date. This may not be the best "plan" for you; disabilities, work demands, and physical or emotional limitations can hinder the best-laid plans to continue working.

However, if it is physically possible for you, this is one considerable way to help your assets last for more than one reason.

In fact, 55 percent of the Americans responding to a survey report they plan to work part-time after retiring, while 15 percent expect compensation from work to be their primary source of retirement income.[34]

I often lean on Dan Sullivan, founder and president of The Strategic Coach, for his wisdom. Dan contends that the problem isn't the problem. The real problem is people don't know how to think about the problem.

Let's take retirement as an example. It's not a problem in itself. The problem is someone's lack of knowledge and understanding regarding retirement planning. They struggle to grasp the concepts that will help them to retire successfully. One of my fellow advisors told me of a lady who came into his office recently. She was about sixty years old. She had saved $5,000 for retirement. When he asked her what she planned to live on in retirement, she said, "the interest."

She was certainly unaware of retirement variables. But often, people are aware; they are only scared.

We attempt to alleviate those concerns with a process we call Six Steps to Retirement Confidence. Each step serves as a handle to help you get a grip on your retirement journey. The first handle is the income step. Do you have enough income to last until age 100? It's not uncommon for individuals to assume they can retire, only to realize through our meticulous calculations that they could fall short of income.

However, we offer strategies and tools that can extend the lifespan of their money by as much as fifteen years. Through that process, people can retire and be less worried about running out of funds. Interestingly enough, once you tell people they can retire, they often hesitate. Retirement isn't everyone's

---

[34] Kerry Hannon. Yahoo! Finance. July 15, 2023. "Future retirees plan to work longer, partly due to savings shortfalls"
https://finance.yahoo.com/news/future-retirees-plan-to-work-longer-partly-due-to-savings-shortfalls-160038419.html

desire, after all. However, we design income plans so that when you decide to retire, you can do so confidently.

When you're retired, you no longer have an employer paying you a steady check. It is up to you to make sure you have saved and planned for the income you need.

CHAPTER 5

Social Security

Social Security is often the foundation of retirement income. Backed by the strength of the U.S. Treasury, it provides perhaps the most dependable paycheck you will have in retirement.

From the time you collect your first paycheck from the job that made you a bona fide taxpayer (for me, it was working as a ticket agent for the Ozark Empire Fair), you are paying into the grand old Social Security system. What grew and developed out of the pressures of the Great Depression has become one of the most popular government programs in the country, and if you pay in for the equivalent of ten years or more, you, too, can benefit from the Social Security program.

Now, before we get into the nitty-gritty of Social Security, I'd like to address a current concern: Will Social Security still be there for you when you reach retirement age?

The Future of Social Security

This question is ever-present as headlines trumpet an underfunded Social Security program, alongside the sea of baby boomers retiring in droves and the comparatively smaller pool of younger people who are funding the system.

The Social Security Administration itself acknowledges this concern as each Social Security statement now contains a link to its website (ssa.gov) and a page entitled, "Will Social Security Be There For Me?"

Just a reminder, as if you needed one, that nothing in life is guaranteed. Additionally, depending on who you're listening to, Social Security funds may run low before 2034, thanks to the financial instability and government spending that accompanied the 2020 COVID-19 pandemic.

Before you get too discouraged, though, here are a few thoughts to keep you going:

- Even if the program is only paying 75 to 78 cents on the dollar for scheduled benefits, this is notably not zero.
- The Social Security Administration has made changes in the distant and near past to help protect the fund's solvency, including increasing retirement ages and striking certain filing strategies.
- There are many changes Congress could make, and lawmakers routinely discuss ideas for amending the system, such as further increasing full retirement age and eligibility.
- One thing no one is seriously discussing? Reneging on current obligations to retirees or the soon-to-retire.

Take heart. The real answer to the question, "Will Social Security be there for me?" is still yes.

This question is important to consider when you look at how much we, as a nation, rely on this program. Did you know Social Security benefits replace about 37 percent of a person's original income when they retire?[35]

If you ask me, that's a pretty significant piece of your retirement income puzzle.

Another caveat? You may not realize this, but the Social Security Administration won't technically "advise" you about your Social Security benefits.

---

[35] Center on Budget and Policy Priorities. April 17, 2023. "Top Ten Facts About Social Security"
https://www.cbpp.org/sites/default/files/atoms/files/8-8-16socsec.pdf

"But, Barry," you may be thinking, what about that nice gentleman at the Social Security Administration office I spoke with on the phone?"

Don't get me wrong. Social Security Administration employees know their stuff. They are trained to understand policies and programs, and they are usually pretty quick to tell you what you can and cannot do. But the Social Security Administration specifically prevents their employees from guiding you in the Social Security claiming process.

But when you work with a retirement planning expert worth their salt, they will know what withdrawal strategies might pertain to your specific situation and will ask questions that can help you determine the best options to choose from so you can make the Social Security claiming decision that best suits your personal situation.

For instance, some people want the highest possible monthly benefit. Others want to start their benefits early, and not always because of financial need. I heard about one man who called in to start his Social Security payments the day he qualified just because he liked to think of it as the government paying back a debt it owed him, and he enjoyed the feeling of receiving a check from Uncle Sam.

Whatever your reasons, questions, or feelings regarding Social Security, the decision is yours alone, but working with a financial professional can help you put your options in perspective by showing you — both with industry knowledge and with proprietary software or planning processes — where your benefits fit into your overall strategy for retirement income.

Full Retirement Age

When it comes to Social Security, it seems like many people only think so far as "yes." They don't take the time to understand the various options available. Instead, because it is common knowledge you can begin your benefits at age sixty-two, that's what many of us do. While more people are opting to delay taking benefits, age sixty-two is still a popular age to start.[36]

Some people fail to understand that starting benefits early may leave significant money on the table. You see, the Social Security Administration bases your monthly benefit on two factors: your earnings history and your full retirement age (FRA).

From your earnings history, the SSA pulls the thirty-five years you made the most money and uses a mathematical indexing formula to figure out a monthly average from those years. If you paid into the system for less than thirty-five years, then every year you didn't pay in will be counted as a zero.

Once they have calculated what your monthly earnings would be at FRA, the government then calculates what to put on your check based on how close you are to FRA. FRA was originally set at sixty-five, but as the population aged and lifespans lengthened, the government shifted FRA later and later, based on an individual's year of birth. Check out the following chart to see when you will reach FRA.[37]

---

[36] Emily Brandon, Erica Sandberg. U.S. News & World Report. August 14, 2023. "The Most Popular Ages to Collect Social Security" https://money.usnews.com/money/retirement/social-security/articles/the-most-popular-ages-to-collect-social-security

[37] Social Security Administration. 2024. "Starting Your Retirement Benefits Early" https://www.ssa.gov/benefits/retirement/planner/agereduction.html

Age to Receive Full Social Security Benefits*

(Called "full retirement age" [FRA] or "normal retirement age.")

Year of Birth*	FRA
1937 or earlier	65
1938	65 and 2 months
1939	65 and 4 months
1940	65 and 6 months
1941	65 and 8 months
1942	65 and 10 months
1943-1954	66
1955	66 and 2 months
1956	66 and 4 months
1957	66 and 6 months
1958	66 and 8 months
1959	66 and 10 months
1960 and later	67

If you were born on January 1 of any year, you should refer to the previous year. (If you were born on the 1st of the month, we figure your benefit [and your full retirement age] as if your birthday was in the previous month.)[38]

When you reach FRA, you are eligible to receive 100 percent of whatever the Social Security Administration calculates as your full monthly benefit.

Starting at age sixty-two, for every year before FRA you claim benefits, your monthly check is reduced by 5 percent or more. Conversely, for every year you delay taking benefits past FRA, your monthly benefit increases by 8 percent (until age seventy — after that, there is no monetary advantage to delaying Social Security benefits). While your circumstances and needs may vary, a lot of financial professionals still urge people to at least consider delaying until they reach age seventy.

Why wait?[39]

Taking benefits early could affect your monthly check by _____.								
62	63	64	65	66	FRA 67	68	69	70
-30%	-25%	-20%	-13.3%	-6.7%	0	+8%	+16%	+24%

[40]

My Social Security

If you are over thirty, you have probably received a notice from the Social Security Administration telling you to activate something called "My Social Security." This is a handy way to learn more about your particular benefit options, keep track of your earnings record, and calculate the benefits you have accrued over the years.

Essentially, My Social Security is an online account you can activate to see your personal Social Security picture. You can

---

[38] Social Security Administration. 2024. "Normal Retirement Age" https://www.ssa.gov/oact/progdata/nra.html
[39] Social Security Administration. 2024. "Retirement Benefits" https://www.ssa.gov/pubs/EN-05-10035.pdf
[40] Social Security Administration. 2024. "Effect of Early or Delayed Retirement on Retirement Benefits" https://www.ssa.gov/oact/ProgData/ar_drc.html

access this information at www.ssa.gov/myaccount. This can be extremely helpful when it comes to planning for income in retirement and figuring out the difference between your anticipated income and anticipated expenses.

COLA

Social Security is a largely guaranteed piece of the retirement puzzle: If you get a statement that reads you should expect $1,000 a month, you can be sure you will receive $1,000 a month. But there is one variable detail, and that is something called the cost-of-living adjustment (COLA).

The COLA is an increase in your monthly check meant to address inflation in everyday life. After all, your expenses will likely continue to experience inflation in retirement, but you will no longer have the opportunity for raises, bonuses, or promotions you had when you were working. Instead, Social Security receives an annual cost-of-living increase tied to the Department of Labor's Consumer Price Index for Urban Wage Earners and Clerical Workers (CPI-W). If the CPI-W measurement shows inflation rose a certain amount for regular goods and services, then Social Security recipients will see that reflected in their COLA.

COLA adjustments have climbed as high as 14.3 percent (1980), and in 2023, they reached 8.7 percent — the largest increase in more than forty years. In a no- or low-inflation environment (such as in 2010, 2011, and 2016), Social Security recipients will not receive an adjustment.[41] The 2024 adjustment decreased to 3.2 percent.[42] Some view the COLA as a perk, bump, or bonus, but in reality, it works more like this: Your mom sends you to the store with $2.50 for a gallon of milk. Milk costs exactly $2.50. The next week, you go back with that same amount, but it is now $2.52 for a gallon, so you go back to

---

[41] Social Security Administration. 2024. "Cost-Of-Living Adjustments" ssa.gov/oact/cola/colaseries.html
[42] Social Security Administration. 2024. "Cost-of-Living Adjustment (COLA) Information for 2024" https://www.ssa.gov/cola/

Mom, and she gives you 2 cents. You aren't bringing home more milk — it just costs more money.

The COLA is less about "making more money" and more about keeping seniors' purchasing power from eroding when inflation is a big factor. Still, don't let that detract from your enthusiasm about COLAs. After all, what if Mom's solution was: "Here's the same $2.50. Try to find pennies from somewhere else to get that milk!"?

Spousal Benefits

We've talked about FRA, but another big Social Security decision involves spousal benefits.

If you or your spouse has a long stretch of zeros in your earnings history — perhaps if one of you stayed home for years, caring for children or sick relatives — you may want to consider filing for spousal benefits instead of filing on your own earnings history. A spousal benefit can be up to 50 percent of the primary wage earner's benefit at full retirement age.

To begin drawing a spousal benefit, you must be at least sixty-two years old, and the primary wage earner must have already filed for their benefit. While there are penalties for taking spousal benefits early, you cannot earn credits for delaying past full retirement age.[43]

As I wrote, the spousal benefit can be a big deal for those who don't have a very long pay history, but it's important to weigh your own earned benefits against the option of withdrawing based on a fraction of your spouse's benefits.

To look at how this could play out, let's use a hypothetical couple: Mary Jane, who is sixty, and Peter, who is sixty-two.

Let's say Peter's benefit at FRA — in his case, sixty-seven — would be $1,600. If Peter begins his benefits right now (five years before FRA), his monthly check will be $1,120. If Mary Jane begins taking spousal benefits in two years at the earliest

---

[43] Social Security Administration. 2024. "Benefits For Your Family" https://www.ssa.gov/benefits/retirement/planner/applying7.html

date possible, her monthly benefits will be reduced to $392 per month (remember, at FRA, the most she can qualify for is half of Peter's FRA benefit).

What if Peter and Mary Jane both wait until FRA? At sixty-seven, Peter begins taking his full benefit of $1,600 a month. Two years later, when she reaches age sixty-seven, Mary Jane will qualify for $800 a month. By waiting until FRA, the couple's monthly benefit goes from $1,512 to $2,400.

What if Peter delays until age seventy to get his maximum possible benefit? For each year past FRA he delays, his monthly benefits increase by 8 percent. This means that at seventy, he could file for a monthly benefit of $1,984. However, delayed retirement credits do not affect spousal benefits, so as soon as Peter files at seventy, Mary Jane would also file (at age sixty-eight) for her maximum benefit of $800, so their highest possible combined monthly check is $2,784.[44]

When it comes to your Social Security benefits, you obviously will want to consider whether a monthly check based on a fraction of your spouse's earnings will be comparable to or larger than your own earnings history.

Divorced Spouses

There are a few considerations for those of us who have gone through a divorce. If you 1) were married for ten years or more *and* 2) have since been divorced for at least two years *and* 3) are unmarried *and* 4) your ex-spouse qualifies to begin Social Security, you qualify for a spousal benefit based on your ex-spouse's earnings history at FRA. A divorced spousal benefit is different from the married spousal benefit in one way: You don't have to wait for your ex-spouse to file before you can file yourself.[45]

---

[44] Social Security Administration. 2024. "Social Security Benefits" https://www.ssa.gov/OACT/quickcalc/spouse.html#calculator
[45] Social Security Administration. 2024. "Benefits For Your Family" https://www.ssa.gov/benefits/retirement/planner/applying7.html

For instance, Charles and Moira were married for fifteen years before their divorce, when he was thirty-six and she was forty. Moira has been remarried for twenty years, and although Charles briefly remarried, his second marriage ended after a few years. Charles' benefits are largely calculated based on his many years of volunteering in schools, meaning his personal monthly benefit is close to zero.

Although Moira has deferred her retirement (opting to delay benefits until she is seventy), Charles can begin taking benefits calculated from Moira's work history at FRA as early as sixty-two. However, he will also have the option of waiting until FRA to collect the maximum, or 50 percent of Moira's earned monthly benefit at her FRA.

Widowed Spouses

If your marriage ended with the death of your spouse, you might claim a benefit for your spouse's earned income as their widow/widower called a survivor's benefit. Unlike spousal benefits or divorced benefits, if your spouse dies, you can claim their full benefit. Also, unlike spousal benefits, you can begin taking income when you turn sixty if you need to. However, as with other benefit options, your monthly check will be permanently reduced for withdrawing benefits before FRA.

If your spouse began taking benefits before they died, you can't delay withdrawing your survivor's benefits to get delayed credits. The Social Security Administration maintains you can only get as much from a survivor's benefit as your deceased spouse might have received had they lived.[46]

Taxes, Taxes, Taxes

With Social Security — as with everything — it is important to consider taxes. It may be surprising, but your Social Security

---

[46] Social Security Administration. 2024. "Receiving Survivors Benefits Early" https://www.ssa.gov/planners/survivors/survivorchartred.html

benefits are not tax-free. Despite having been taxed to accrue those benefits in the first place, you may have to pay Uncle Sam income taxes on up to 85 percent of your Social Security.

The Social Security Administration figures these taxes using what they call "the provisional income formula." Your provisional income formula differs from the adjusted gross income you use for your regular income taxes. Instead, to find out how much of your Social Security benefit is taxable, the Social Security Administration calculates it this way:

Provisional Income = Adjusted Gross Income + Nontaxable Interest + ½ of Social Security

See that piece about nontaxable interest? That generally means interest from government bonds and notes. It surprises many people that although you may not pay taxes on those assets, their income will count against you when it comes to Social Security taxation.

Once you have figured out your provisional income (also called "combined income"), you can use the following chart to figure out your Social Security taxes.[47]

---

[47] Julia Kagan. Investopedia. October 8, 2022. "Provisional Taxes: What They are and how They Work"
https://www.investopedia.com/terms/p/provisional-income.asp

Taxes on Social Security

Provisional Income = Adjusted Gross Income + Nontaxable Interest + ½ of Social Security

If you are ___ and your provisional income is___, then ...		Uncle Sam will tax ___ of your Social Security
Single	Married, filing jointly	
Less than $25,000	Less than $32,000	0%
$25,000 to $34,000	$32,000 to $44,000	Up to 50%
More than $34,000	More than $44,000	Up to 85%

[48]

This is one more reason why working with financial and tax professionals may benefit you. They can help you look at your entire financial picture to make your overall retirement plan as tax-efficient as possible — including your Social Security benefit.

Deciphering the tax implications of Social Security can profoundly influence your retirement strategy. The pivotal factor is your provisional income, which is a blend of assorted income streams that determines the taxability of your Social Security benefits. It's essential to grasp this concept for a financially secure retirement.

For married couples with a combined yearly income exceeding $44,000, 85 percent of Social Security benefits become taxable. While 85 percent is taxable, it isn't the tax rate. Rather, it signifies that 85 cents of every dollar received from Social Security will be taxed at your marginal rate.

---

[48] Ibid.

To avoid taxes on Social Security, aim to maintain your taxable income below this threshold. The IRS assesses taxability using "provisional income," which includes:

- W-2 income from employment
- 1099 income, encompassing bank interest and other sources
- K-1 income from partnership stakes, investments, or rental properties
- Withdrawals from IRAs or 401(k)s
- Tax-exempt interest, typically from municipal bonds
- 50 percent of your Social Security benefits

The grand total of these streams dictates if — and how much — your Social Security will be taxed. The strategy lies in orienting your income to stem from sources other than the standard 1099, K-1, W-2, etc., formats.

In our practice, we advocate for a "three-bucket" approach to income planning: taxable, tax-deferred, and tax-free. The latter features instruments such as Roth conversions, Roth 401(k)s, Roth IRAs, or Section 7702 Life Insurance Retirement Plans (LIRPs), all of which are excluded from the provisional income total.

By meticulously positioning your assets well in advance and leveraging these tax-advantaged avenues, it's plausible to draw significant income while keeping your Social Security benefits completely tax-free. This effective allocation ensures that your income stems from sources that don't trip the IRS' "provisional income" sensors.

Working and Social Security: The Earnings Test

If you haven't reached FRA but you started your Social Security benefits and are still working, things get a little hairy.

Because you have started Social Security payments, the Social Security Administration will pay out your benefits (at that reduced rate, of course, because you haven't reached your FRA). Yet, because you are working, the organization must also withhold from your check to add to your benefits, which you are already collecting. See how this complicates matters?

To address the situation, the government has what is called the earnings test. For 2024, you can earn up to $22,320 without it affecting your Social Security check if you're younger than full retirement age. But, for every $2 you earn past that amount, the Social Security Administration will withhold $1. The earnings test loosens in the year of your FRA; if you are reaching FRA in 2024, you can earn up to $59,520 before you run into the earnings test, and the government only withholds $1 for every $3 past that amount.

The month you reach FRA, you are no longer subject to any earnings withholding. For instance, if you are still working and will turn sixty-seven on December 28, 2024, you would only have to worry about the earnings test until December, and then you can ignore it entirely. Keep in mind, the money the government withholds from your Social Security benefits while you are working before FRA will be tacked back onto your benefits check after FRA.[49]

Railroad Retirement Benefits

The Railroad Retirement Act was established in 1934 to address concerns about existing pension programs' ability to provide former railroad employees with old-age benefits.[50] The Act continues to provide benefits to retired and disabled workers, and their dependents, based on their length of employment in the industry. Although there are similarities to Social Security,

---

[49] Social Security Administration. 2024. "Receiving Benefits While Working"
https://www.ssa.gov/benefits/retirement/planner/whileworking.html
[50] U.S. Railroad Retirement Board. January, 2023. "2023 Agency Overview"
https://www.rrb.gov/OurAgency/AgencyOverview

there are considerable differences, which include payment amounts, eligibility age, and taxation obligations.

Like Social Security, Railroad Retirement Benefits (RRB) are funded from payroll taxes of current employees and employers. Also, both types of benefits are received by retirees as a monthly check. RRBs use the same formula to calculate COLAs as Social Security.

The differences between the two retirement programs are intricate. The average monthly RRB payment is more generous than Social Security because railroad workers pay higher taxes into the program. Another major difference is the age at which railroad workers are eligible to begin collecting benefits: A railroad worker with thirty or more years of service is eligible for full benefits at age sixty without a reduction.

The taxation of RRBs is more complex than Social Security payments. To determine the tax, RRBs are broken down into two components:
- Tier I benefits resemble Social Security, a private pension, or a combination of both
- Tier II benefits are similar to a private pension[51]

The portion of the Tier I benefit equivalent to Social Security is taxed the same way as Social Security benefits, but the portion not equivalent is fully taxable. Regarding the Tier II, a portion is always taxable and subject to ordinary income tax rates.[52]

Deciding when to claim Social Security benefits is a critical financial decision that requires thoughtful consideration and strategic planning. Unfortunately, the answer is never simple

---

[51] Kurt Woock. NerdWallet. February 7, 2024. "Railroad Retirement Board: What It Is, How It Works"
https://www.nerdwallet.com/article/investing/social-security/what-is-the-railroad-retirement-board

[52] True Tamplin. Finance Strategists. September 7, 2023. "Is Railroad Retirement Income Taxable?"
https://www.financestrategists.com/retirement-planning/retirement-income-planning/is-railroad-retirement-income-taxable/

and straightforward because we do not know precisely how long we will live.

Often, people claim benefits as soon as they become eligible at age sixty-two. They can be influenced by societal norms rather than a personalized financial strategy. However, it is vital to recognize that claiming earlier reduces monthly benefits. Deferring benefits up to age seventy can significantly increase benefits due to the delayed retirement credits, resulting in an 8 percent annual increase.

The question of when exactly to claim benefits doesn't come with a one-size-fits-all answer — it depends on individual circumstances. Your decision should hinge on several factors, including anticipated longevity, health status, other income streams, and spousal benefits, all of which play a role in optimizing one's overall financial picture.

To navigate this decision, it's imperative to undergo a comprehensive analysis that takes into account life expectancy, other sources of retirement income, and the potential implications for a surviving spouse. An informed approach involves comparing scenarios: the implications of early retirement, full retirement age based on your birth year, and delayed retirement.

This process can illuminate the potential long-term benefits and drawbacks, ensuring that when you decide to take Social Security, it aligns with your overall retirement goals. With proper guidance and a clear understanding of these dynamics, individuals can structure their Social Security benefits as part of a robust retirement strategy.

CHAPTER 6
401(k)s, IRAs, and Roth IRAs

Have you heard? Today's retirement is not your parents' retirement. You see, back in the day, it was pretty common to work for one company for the vast majority of your career and then retire with a gold watch and a pension.

The gold watch was a symbol of the quality time you had put in at that company, but the pension was more than a symbol. Instead, it was a guarantee — as solid as your employer — that they would repay your hard work with a certain amount of income in your old age. Did you see the caveat there? Your pension's guarantee was *as solid as your employer.* The problem was, what if your employer went under?

Companies that failed couldn't pay their retired employees' pensions, leading to financial challenges for many. Beginning in 1974 with Congress' passage of the Employee Retirement Income Security Act, federal legislation and regulations aimed at protecting retirees were everywhere. One piece of legislation included a relatively obscure section of the Internal Revenue Code, added in 1978 — Section 401(k), to be specific.

IRC section 401, subsection k, created tax advantages for employer-sponsored financial products, even if the main contributor was the employee themselves. Over the years, more employers took note, beginning an age of transition away from pensions and toward 401(k) plans. A 401(k) is a retirement account with certain tax benefits and restrictions on the investments or other financial products inside of it.

Essentially, 401(k)s and their individual retirement account (IRA) counterparts are "wrappers" that provide tax benefits around assets; typically, the assets that compose IRAs and 401(k)s are mutual funds, stock and bond mixes, and money market accounts. However, IRA and 401(k) contents are becoming more diverse these days, with some companies offering different kinds of annuity options within their plans.

Where pensions are defined-*benefit* plans, 401(k)s and IRAs are defined-*contribution* plans. The one-word change outlines the basic difference. Pensions spell out what you can expect to receive from the plan but not necessarily how much money it will take to fund those benefits. With 401(k)s, an employer sets a standard for how much they will contribute (if any), and you can be certain of what you are contributing. Still, there is no outline for what you can expect to receive in return for those contributions.

Modern employment looks very different. A 2022 survey by the Bureau of Labor Statistics determined U.S. workers stayed with their employers for a median of 4.1 years. Workers aged fifty-five to sixty-four had a little more staying power and were most likely to stay with their employer for about ten years.[53] Participation in 401(k) plans appears solid. In a study, Vanguard reported a record plan participation rate of 83 percent in 2022. Plans with automatic enrollment drew a 93 percent participation rate.[54]

Those statistics make it clear that 401(k) plans have replaced pensions at many companies and, for that matter, a gold watch.

If there is anything to learn from this paradigm shift, it's that you must look out for yourself. Whether you have worked for a company for two years or twenty, you are still the one who has to look out for your own best interests. That holds doubly true

---

[53] U.S. Bureau of Labor Statistics. September 22, 2022. "Employee Tenure Summary" https://www.bls.gov/news.release/tenure.nr0.htm
[54] Vanguard. 2023. "How America Saves 2023" https://institutional.vanguard.com/content/dam/inst/iig-transformation/has/2023/pdf/has-insights/how-america-saves-report-2023.pdf

when it comes to preparing for retirement. If you are one of the lucky ones who still has a pension, good for you. But for the rest of us, it is likely a 401(k) — or possibly one of its nonprofit- or government-sector counterparts, a 403(b) or 457 plan — is one of your biggest assets for retirement.

Some employers offer incentives to contribute to their company plans, like a company match. On that subject, I have one thing to say: *Do it!* Nothing in life is free, as they say, but a company match on your retirement funds is about as close to free money as it gets. If you can make the minimum to qualify for your company's match at all, go for it.

Now, it's likely that during our working years, we mostly "set and forget" our 401(k) funding. Because it is tax-advantaged, your employer is taking money from your paycheck — before taxes — and putting it into your plan for you. Maybe you were able to pick a selection of investments, or maybe your company only offers one choice of investment in your 401(k). Either way, while you are gainfully employed, your most impactful decision may just be the decision to continue funding your plan in the first place. But when you are ready to retire or move jobs, you have choices to make requiring a little more thought and care.

When you are ready to part ways with your job, you have a few options:
- Leave the money where it is
- Take the cash (and pay income taxes and perhaps a 10 percent additional federal tax if you are younger than age fifty-nine-and-one-half)
- Transfer the money to another employer plan (if the new plan allows)
- Roll the money over into a self-directed IRA

Now, these are just general options. You will have to decide — hopefully with the help of a financial professional — what's right for you. For instance, 401(k)s are typically pretty closely tied to the companies offering them, so when changing jobs, it may not always be possible to transfer a 401(k) to another

401(k). Leaving the money where it is may also be out of the question — some companies have direct cash payout or rollover policies once someone is no longer employed.

Also, remember what we mentioned earlier about how we change jobs more often these days? That means you likely have a 401(k) with your current company, but you may also have a string of retirement accounts trailing you from other jobs.

We often see people who have busily skipped along their career landscape, leaving a trail of retirement accounts in their wake. It's commonplace for them to maintain separate 401(k)s from every employer, alongside IRAs aligned with numerous brokerage firms as financial strategies shifted. We might discover a dozen or more of these accounts, each requiring attention.

This disjointed financial picture can sometimes seem like tangled fishing line within a knotted reel. Investments can pull in various, perhaps conflicting, directions. The solution? A sweeping consolidation — a spring cleaning of sorts. The goal is to bring together these disparate funds under the roof of one self-directed IRA at a single custodian, enabling a unified and manageable approach to your retirement strategy.

Consolidation also provides the opportunity to align your beneficiary designations across the board. It's startling how often we find accounts unintentionally bequeathed to outdated beneficiaries — a relic from first marriages or to people who have long passed, while current loved ones are sometimes left out. A beneficiary audit is in order and something our company conducts immediately with any new client.

Our advice is to streamline — merge those accounts, ensure your beneficiaries reflect your current wishes, and develop a retirement plan with coherence and foresight. A tidy retirement plan is not just about consolidating for convenience. It's about paving a clear path to your future financial security.

We want to guide you towards a configuration that cements control over your investments, secures your legacy in accordance with your current life stage, and eliminates the chaos of scattered financial accounts. This attention to detail transforms the retirement journey from a daunting quest into a navigable venture.

When it comes to your retirement income, it's important to be able to pull together *all* your assets, so you can examine what you have and where, and then decide what you will do with it.

Tax-Qualified, Tax-Preferred, Tax-Deferred ... Still TAXED

Financial media often cite IRAs and 401(k)s for their tax benefits. After all, with traditional plans, you put your money in pre-tax, and it hopefully grows for years — even decades — untaxed. That's why these accounts are called "tax-qualified" or "tax-deferred" assets. They aren't *tax-free!* Rarely does Uncle Sam allow business to continue without receiving his piece of the pie, and your retirement assets are no different. If you didn't pay taxes on the front end, you will pay taxes on the money you withdraw from these accounts in retirement. Don't get me wrong: This isn't an inherently good or bad thing; it's just the way it is. It's important to understand, though, for the sake of planning ahead.

In retirement, many people assume they will be in a lower tax bracket. As referenced in the Taxes chapter, for retirees with healthy balances in tax-deferred assets, their retirement marginal tax rate may be the same or even more than their pre-retirement rate. The timing involved with beginning Social Security or in shifting or converting funds out of tax-deferred assets is of strategic concern because of taxes owed on those assets.

Keep in mind, IRAs, 401(k)s, and their alternatives have a few limitations because of their special tax status. For one thing, the IRS sets limits on your contributions to these retirement accounts. If you are contributing to a 401(k) or an equivalent nonprofit or government plan, your annual contribution limit is $23,000 (as of 2024). If you are fifty or older, the IRS allows additional contributions, called "catch-up contributions," of up to $7,500 on top of the regular limit of $23,000. For an IRA, the limit is $7,000, with a catch-up limit of an additional $1,000.[55] Beginning in 2026, catch-up contributions for individuals with income exceeding $145,000 must transfer into a Roth IRA.[56]

Because their tax advantages come from their intended use as retirement income, withdrawing funds from these accounts before you turn fifty-nine-and-one-half can carry stiff penalties. In addition to fees your investment management company might charge, you will have to pay income tax *and* a 10 percent federal tax penalty, with a few exceptions.

The fifty-nine-and-one-half rule for retirement accounts is incredibly important to remember, especially when you're young. Younger workers are often tempted to cash out an IRA from a previous employer and then are surprised to find their checks missing 20 percent of the account value to income taxes, penalty taxes, and account fees.

Many millennials I see in my practice say that while they may be socking money away in their workplace retirement plan, it is often the *only* place they are saving. This could be problematic later because of the fifty-nine-and-one-half rule; what if you have an emergency? It is important to fund your retirement, but you need to have some liquid assets handy as emergency funds. This can help you avoid breaking into your retirement accounts and incurring taxes and penalties because of the fifty-nine-and-one-half rule.

---

[55] Fidelity. March 4, 2024. "IRA contribution limits for 2023 and 2024" https://www.fidelity.com/learning-center/smart-money/ira-contribution-limits

[56] Robert Powell. The Street. September 11, 2023. "Ask the Hammer: Catch-up Contributions Now Permitted Until 2026" https://www.thestreet.com/retirement-daily/ask-the-hammer/catch-up-contributions-now-permitted-until-2026

RMDs

Remember how we talked about the 401(k) or IRA being a "tax wrapper" for your funds? Well, eventually, Uncle Sam will want a bite of that candy bar. So, when you turn seventy-three, the government requires you to withdraw a portion of your account, which the IRS calculates based on the size of your account and your estimated lifespan. This required minimum distribution (RMD) is the government's insurance it will collect some taxes from your earnings at some point. Because you didn't pay taxes on the front end, you will now pay income taxes on whatever you withdraw — including your RMDs.

Let me reiterate something I pointed out in the Longevity chapter. Beginning at age seventy-three, you are required to withdraw a certain minimum amount every year from your 401(k) or IRA, or else you will face a tax penalty on any RMD monies you should have withdrawn but didn't — and that's on top of income tax. The SECURE Act 2.0 reduced the penalty to 25 percent (from 50 percent). Timely corrections also can reduce the penalty to 10 percent.[57]

Even after you begin RMDs, you can still continue contributing to your 401(k) or IRAs if you are still employed, which can affect the whole discussion on RMDs and possible tax considerations. The SECURE Act 2.0 raised the RMD age to seventy-three from seventy-two. In addition, the latest legislation stipulates the RMD age will increase to seventy-five for those turning seventy-four after December 31, 2032.[58]

If you don't need income from your retirement accounts, RMDs can seem like more of a tax burden than an income boon. While some people prefer to reinvest their RMDs, this comes with the possibility of additional taxation: You'll pay income taxes on your RMDs and then potential capital gains taxes on

---

[57] Jim Probasco. Investopedia. January 6, 2023. "SECURE 2.0 Act of 2022" https://www.investopedia.com/secure-2-0-definition-5225115
[58] Ibid.

the growth of your investments. If you are legacy-minded, there are other ways to use RMDs, many of which have tax benefits.

SECURE 2.0 Act provisions

In addition to changes imposed for RMD ages, Secure Act 2.0 also expanded access to retirement savings using different methods. Provisions in the legislation go into effect at different times, ranging from 2023-25.

- Beginning January 2, 2024, plan participants can access up to $1,000 (once a year) from retirement savings for emergency, personal, or family expenses without paying a 10 percent early-withdrawal penalty.
- Beginning January 2, 2024, employees can establish a Roth emergency savings account of up to $2,500 per participant.
- Beginning January 2, 2024, domestic abuse survivors can withdraw the lesser of $10,000 or 50 percent of their retirement account without penalty.[59]
- Beginning January 1, 2023, victims of a qualified, federally declared disaster can withdraw up to $22,000 from their retirement account without penalty.[60]

Permanent Life Insurance

One way to turn those pesky RMDs into a legacy is through permanent life insurance. Assuming you need the death benefit coverage and can qualify for it medically, if properly structured, these products can pass on a sizeable death benefit to your beneficiaries — tax-free — as part of your general legacy plan.

---

[59] Betterment editors. Betterment. February 24, 2023. "SECURE Act 2.0: Signed into Law" https://www.betterment.com/work/resources/secure-act-2

[60] Charlie Pastor. The Motley Fool. February 16, 2023. "Law Opens New Doors for Penalty-Free Retirement Account Distributions" www.fool.com/the-ascent/buying-stocks/articles/law-opens-new-doors-for-penalty-free-retirement-account-distributions

ILIT
Another way to use RMDs toward your legacy is to work with an estate planning attorney to create an irrevocable life insurance trust (ILIT). This is basically a permanent life insurance policy placed within a trust. Because the trust is irrevocable, you would relinquish control of it, but unlike with just a permanent life insurance policy, your death benefit won't count toward your taxable estate.

Annuities
Because annuities can be tax-deferred, using all or a portion of your RMDs to fund an annuity contract can be one way to further delay taxation while guaranteeing your income payments (either to you or your loved ones) later. Of course, this assumes you don't need the RMD income during your retirement.

Qualified Charitable Distributions
If you are charity-minded, you may use your RMDs toward a charitable organization instead of using them for income. You must do this directly from your retirement account (you can't take the RMD check and *then* pay the charity) for your withdrawals to be qualified charitable distributions (QCDs), but this is one way of realizing some of the benefits of a charitable legacy during your own lifetime. You will not need to pay taxes on your QCDs, and they won't count toward your annual charitable tax deduction limit, plus you'll be able to see how the organization you are supporting uses your donations. You should consult a financial professional on how to correctly make a QCD.

As a longstanding client familiar with our strategies, you're likely to witness the power of proactive planning. With our guidance, it's possible that you'll bypass those pesky required minimum distributions (RMDs) altogether, thanks to strategic placement of your assets into tax-exempt vehicles. Even for those who partner with us later in their financial journey, achieving a complete tax-free status in the early stages of RMDs is a plausible goal.

Let's face the music: taxes are inevitable. However, it is better to tackle them on your own terms, early, while tax rates are at historically low levels. Through different strategies, we can harness credits to counterbalance the tax bite, ensuring you part with your hard-earned cash in a manner and at a rate that you dictate rather than leaving it up to the taxman.

If you sit idly by, you give up control of when, how much, and at what cost your RMDs will be paid out. Taking command of your financial future is critical. So, why wait and forfeit control? Your retirement need not be a time of uncertainty but rather a continuation of the informed and deliberate decisions that you've made all along.

Roth IRA

Since the Taxpayer Relief Act of 1997, there has been a different kind of retirement account — or "tax wrapper" — available to the public: the Roth. Roth IRAs and Roth 401(k)s each differ from their traditional counterparts in one big way: You pay your taxes on the front end. Once your post-tax money is in the Roth account, as long as you follow the rules and limitations of that account, your distributions are truly tax-free. You won't pay income tax when you take withdrawals, so in turn, you don't have to worry about RMDs. However, Roth accounts have the same limitations as traditional 401(k)s and IRAs when it comes to withdrawing money before age fifty-nine-and-one-half, with the added stipulation that the account must have been open for at least five years for the account holder to make withdrawals.

Roth conversions can be a strategic move financially, and something we execute for many of our clients. However, we must approach any situation wisely.

If your current position finds you comfortably within, say, the 22 percent tax bracket, there's a strategic opportunity –

moving assets from your traditional IRA to a Roth IRA. This process, termed a *conversion*, is essentially opting to pay taxes early, circumventing the financial strain of future tax hikes.

How should one determine the optimal amount for conversion? It boils down to understanding your proximity to the top of your existing tax bracket. If you're nearing that cap – perhaps 80 percent of the way there – it's prudent to leverage the remaining space. For example, by topping up to the peak of the 22 percent bracket, you smartly convert funds without jumping to the next level.

However, when that next level is a marginal increase to a 24 percent bracket, the distinction might seem nominal. Despite a seemingly negligible 2 percent hike, precision is key; erring on the side of caution is advised rather than oversimplifying. Our goal would be to fill that 24 percent as well, ensuring each conversion maximizes your advantage without inducing what we call *tax shock*.

But why not dare to convert at even higher rates – up to 35 percent? This is where the law of diminishing returns could come into play. Crossing that threshold may not benefit you as much. Before we cross it, we want to be sure it benefits you to pay taxes at that rate, or that we had a compensating strategy that can offset those taxes so we don't lead you to unnecessarily pay taxes at a higher rate than would be beneficial to you over the long term. The objective is to find the optimal conversion point.

Taking Charge

As mentioned earlier, the 401(k) and IRA have largely replaced pensions, but they aren't an equal trade.

Pensions are employer-funded; the money feeding into them is money that wouldn't ever show up on your pay stub. Because 401(k)s are self-funded, you must actively and consciously save. This distinction has made a difference when it comes to funding retirement. Fidelity Investments published a study detailing the average 401(k) balance for a person aged fifty-five to sixty-four is $207,874, but the median likely tells the full story. The median 401(k) balance for a person aged fifty-five to sixty-four is $71,168. Those figures reflect Fidelity accounts from the third quarter of 2024.[61]

There can be many reasons why people underfund their retirement plans, like being overwhelmed by investment choices or taking withdrawals from IRAs when they leave an employer. Still, the reason at the top of the list seems to be this: People simply aren't participating to begin with.

So, whether you use a 401(k) with an employer or an IRA alternative with a private company separate from your workplace, the most important retirement savings decision you can make is to sock away your money somewhere in the first place.

---

[61] Arielle O'Shea and Elizabeth Ayoola. NerdWallet. February 16, 2024. "The Average 401(k) Balance by Age"
https://www.nerdwallet.com/article/investing/the-average-401k-balance-by-age

CHAPTER 7
Annuities

In my practice, I offer my clients a variety of products — from securities to insurance — designed to help them work toward their financial goals. You may be wondering: Why single out a single product in this book?

Well, while most of my clients have a pretty good understanding of business and finance, I sometimes find those who have the impression magic must be involved. Some people assume there is a magic finance wand we can wave to change years' worth of savings into a strategy for retirement income. But it's not as easy as a goose laying golden eggs or the Fairy Godmother turning a pumpkin into a coach!

Finances aren't magic; it takes lots of hard work and, typically, several financial products and strategies to pull together a complete retirement plan. Of all the financial products I work with, it seems people find none more mysterious than annuities. And, if I may say, even some of those who recognize the word "annuity" have a limited understanding of the product. So, in the interest of demystifying annuities, let me tell you a little about what an annuity is.

In general, insurance is a financial hedge against risk. Car owners buy auto insurance to protect their finances in case they injure someone or someone injures them. Homeowners have house insurance to protect their finances in case of a fire, flood, or another disaster. People have life insurance to protect their finances in case of untimely death. Almost juxtaposed to life insurance, people have annuities in case of a long life; annuities can give you financial protection by providing consistent and reliable income payments.

The basic premise of an annuity is you, the annuitant, pay an insurance company some amount in exchange for their contractual guarantee they will pay you income for a certain time period. How that company pays you, for how long, and how much they offer are all determined by the annuity contract you enter into with the insurance company.

The Ways You Get Paid

There are several ways for an annuity contract to provide income: annuitization, income riders, partial surrenders, and settlement options for heirs.

Annuitization

When someone "annuitizes" a contract, it is the point where they turn on the income stream. Once a contract has been annuitized, there is no going back. With annuities, if the policyholder lives longer than the insurance company planned, the insurance company is still obligated to pay them, even if the payments are way more than the contract's actual value.

If, however, the policyholder dies an untimely death, depending on the contract type, the insurance company may keep anything left of the money that funded the annuity. Nothing would be paid out to the contract holder's survivors. You see where that could make some people balk? Now, modern annuities rarely rely on annuitization for the income portion of the contract, and instead have so many bells and whistles that the old concept of annuitization seems outdated, but because this is still an option, it's important to at least understand the basic concept.

Riders

Speaking of bells and whistles, let's talk about riders. Modern annuities have a lot of different options these days, many in the form of riders you can add to your contract for a fee. The fee typically amounts to 0.1 percent to 1 percent of the contract value per year.[62] Each rider has its particulars, and the types of riders available will vary by the type of annuity contract purchased, but I'll just briefly outline some of these little extras:

- Lifetime income rider: Contract guarantees you an enhanced or flexible income for life
- Death benefit rider: Contract pays an enhanced death benefit to your beneficiaries, even if you have annuitized
- Return of premium rider: Guarantees you (or your beneficiaries) will at least receive back the premium value of the annuity
- Long-term care rider: Provides a certain amount, sometimes as much as twice the normal income benefit amount for a period of time to help pay for long-term care if the contract holder is moved to a nursing home or assisted living situation

This isn't an extensive look, and usually the riders have fancier names based on the issuing company, like "XYZ Insurance Company Income Preferred Bonus Fixed Index Annuity rider," but I just wanted to show you what some of the general options are in layperson's terms.

Partial Surrender

Most annuities offer a free withdrawal provision that is often referred to as a partial surrender. An annuity contract typically allows for an annual withdrawal of up to 10 percent, typically,

---

[62] Shawn Plummer. The Annuity Expert. 2024. "Annuity Fees: What You Need To Know" https://www.annuityexpertadvice.com/types-of-annuities/annuity-fees/

of the account value or of the premium originally paid. The option to make this withdrawal, typically without penalty, can be used as a tool to help with your income planning strategies. Keep in mind, the withdrawal is subject to income taxes, and an additional 10 percent IRS penalty if you're under age fifty-nine-and-one-half.

This percentage can be accessed during the surrender period and can be a sound strategy, especially for a client who does not require a regular influx of income provided by a rider. After the surrender value period, the holder of the annuity can access the annuity without losing control of the account value.

I find the partial surrender strategy to often be effective for my clients, particularly if they do not need regular income generated through the use of a rider. A partial surrender allows for the annuity holder to just take out funds when a need arises.

Settlement Options

While any value of an annuity left to beneficiaries upon the annuity holder's death is fairly self-explanatory, there is a point worth raising. Heirs have different settlement options they can consider, including opportunities for lump sums, periodic payments, or specific payouts.

Specific payouts are often based on tax considerations involving a beneficiary or multiple beneficiaries. As an advanced tax planning measure, I have clients who have addressed tax implications with their heirs regarding the most advantageous method for arranging a settlement option that eases any tax burden on the beneficiary.

Types of Annuities

Annuities break down into four basic types: immediate, variable, fixed, and fixed index.

Immediate

Immediate annuities primarily rely on annuitization to provide income. You give the insurance company a lump sum up front, and your payments begin immediately. Once you begin receiving income payments, the transaction is irreversible, and you no longer have access to your money in a lump sum. When you die, any remaining contract value is typically forfeited to the insurance company.

All other annuity contract types are "deferred" contracts, meaning you fund your policy as a lump sum or over a period of years. You give it the opportunity to grow over time — sometimes years, sometimes decades.

Variable

A variable annuity is an insurance contract as well as a security product. It's sold by insurance companies, but only through someone who is also registered to sell security products. With a variable annuity contract, the insurance company invests your premiums in sub-accounts that are tied to the stock market.

This makes it a bit different from the other annuity contract types because it is the only contract where your money is subject to losses because of market declines. Your contract value has a greater opportunity to grow, but it also stands to lose. Additionally, your contract's value will be subject to the underlying investment's fees and limitations — including capital gains taxes, management fees, etc. Once it is time for you to receive income from the contract, the insurance company will pay you a certain income, locked in at whatever your contract's value was.[*]

---

[*] A variable annuity is sold by prospectus. Carefully read the prospectus before purchasing a variable annuity.

Fixed

A traditional fixed annuity is pretty straightforward. You purchase a contract with a guaranteed interest rate, and when you are ready, the insurance company will make regular income payments to you at whatever payout rate your contract guarantees. Those payments will continue for the rest of your life and, if you choose, for the remainder of your spouse's life.

Fixed annuities don't typically offer significant upside potential, but many people like them for their guarantees and predictability. After all, if your Aunt May lives to be ninety-five, knowing she has a paycheck later in life can be her mental and financial safety net. Unlike variable annuities, which are subject to market risk and might be up one year and down the next, you can easily calculate the value of your fixed annuity over your lifetime.

Fixed Index

To recap, variable annuities take on more risk to offer more possibilities to grow. Fixed annuities have less potential growth, but they protect your principal. In the last couple of decades, many insurance companies have retooled their product line to offer fixed indexed annuities, which are sort of midway between variable and fixed annuities on that risk/reward spectrum. Fixed index annuities offer greater growth potential than traditional fixed annuities but less than variable annuities. Like traditional fixed annuities, however, fixed index annuities are protected from downside market losses.

Fixed index annuities earn interest that is tied to an external market index, meaning that instead of your contract value growing at a set interest rate like a traditional fixed annuity, it has the potential to grow within a range. Your contract's value is credited interest based on the performance of an external market index like the S&P 500® while never being invested in the market itself. You can't invest in the S&P 500® directly, but based on when you contract credits interest to your account (e.g., one year — point-to-point, two years — point-to-point, etc.), your annuity has the potential to earn interest based on the chosen index's performance. The interest is subject to limits set by the company (such as caps, spreads, and participation rates).

For instance, if your contract caps your interest at 5 percent, then in a year that the S&P 500® gains 3 percent, your annuity value increases 3 percent. If the S&P 500® gains 35 percent, your annuity value gets a 5 percent interest bump. But since your money isn't actually invested in the market with a fixed index annuity, if the market nosedives (such as happened during 2000, 2008, 2020, and 2022, anyone?), you won't see any increase in your contract value. Insurance carriers charge Mortality & Expense fees (M&E fees) and may charge additional administrative fees to maintain the insurance policy contract that can lower your contract value. Conversely, there will also be no decrease in your contract value, no matter how badly the market performs. As long as you follow the terms of the contract, you won't lose any of the interest you were credited in previous years.

So, what if the S&P 500® shows a market loss of 30 percent? Your contract value isn't going anywhere unless you purchased an optional rider. This charge will still come out of your annuity value each year, along with M&E fees and possibly administrative fees). For those who are more interested in protection than significant growth potential, fixed index annuities can be an attractive option. When the stock market has a long period of positive performance, a fixed index annuity can enjoy conservative growth. And during stretches where the stock market is erratic and stock values across the board take significant losses? Fixed index annuities won't lose anything due to the stock market volatility.

Other Things to Know About Annuities

We just explained the four kinds of annuity contracts available, but all of them have some commonalities as annuities.

For all annuities, the contractual guarantees are only as strong as the insurance company that sells the product, which makes it important to thoroughly check the credit ratings of any company whose products you are considering.

Annuities are tax-deferred, meaning you don't have to pay taxes on interest earnings each year as the contract value grows. Instead, you will pay ordinary income taxes on your withdrawals. These are meant to be long-term products, so like other tax-deferred or tax-advantaged products, if you begin taking withdrawals from your contract before age fifty-nine-and-one-half, you may also have to pay a 10 percent federal tax penalty. Also, while annuities are generally considered illiquid, some contracts allow you to withdraw up to 10 percent of your contract value every year. Withdraw any more, however, and you could incur additional surrender penalties.

Keep in mind, your withdrawals will deplete the accumulated cash value, death benefit, and possibly the rider values of your contract.

Our business centers on helping clients get what they want. Annuities can be an important part of that recipe for a client who wants the protection of principle. But for people who have a personality, or a situation, that can endure more risk, an annuity might not be appropriate.

When the stock market grows turbulent, I make it a point to reach out to my clients. I engage in reassuring conversations about the strategies and protections we have in place as part of their plan.

I remember one of those calls speaking with a retiree. Before I could say anything, I heard his wife shout in the background, expressing her relief about the protected and guaranteed money they had.

This turned out to be a particularly good decision after the wife received a serious health diagnosis that may impact her lifespan. This reinforced their satisfaction with the choice they made to prioritize principal protection.

Annuities aren't for everyone, but it's important to understand them before saying "yea" or "nay" on whether they fit into your plan; otherwise, you're not operating with complete information, wouldn't you agree? Regardless, you should talk to a financial professional who can help you understand annuities, help you dissect your particular financial needs, and help show you whether an annuity is appropriate for your retirement income plan.

CHAPTER 8

Estate and Legacy Planning Strategies

In my practice, I devote a significant portion of my time to matters of estate and legacy planning strategies. That doesn't mean drawing up wills or trusts or putting together powers of attorney or anything like that. After all, I'm not an estate planning attorney. But I am a financial professional, and what part of the "estate" isn't affected by money matters?

I've included this chapter because I have seen many people do estate planning wrong. Clients, or clients' families, have come in after experiencing a death in the family and have found themselves in the middle of probate, high taxes, or a discovery of something unforeseen (often long-term care) draining the estate.

I have also seen people do estate planning right: clients or families who visit my office to talk about legacies and ways to make them last, and adult children who have room to grieve without an added burden of unintended costs or stress from a family fractured because of inadequate planning.

I'll share some of these stories here. However, I'm not going to give you specific advice, since everyone's situation is unique. I only want to give you some things to think about and to underscore the importance of planning ahead.

We have a staff member who previously worked at an estate planning firm. Although he is not an attorney, he possesses a deep understanding of estate planning. His former firm relied on a document preparation service, which we introduce to our clients for simple cases. We also discuss the option of engaging attorneys if that makes clients more comfortable or they have a situation that is particularly complex and requires more nuanced solutions.

To guide our clients through the process, we assist them in gathering the necessary information, and completing the required documents to communicate their wishes to the attorney drafting their estate planning documents. Once clients receive them, we take the time to thoroughly explain the contents of their documents using clear, definitive language. Ever run across an attorney who breaks into Latin terminology? That's because their training was rooted in ancient language. People we meet don't understand the principles outlined in such nomenclature.

Unfortunately, I have experienced situations where clients possess a trust document but lack a clear understanding of its implications and functionality. They often bring a comprehensive binder containing their trust, yet are unaware of its purpose or how it works. To gauge the extent to which the trust has been established, we inquire about its funding. Astonishingly, the response is often a shrug of the shoulders, suggesting uncertainty.

We carefully examine their documents, questioning whether their property, such as their house, has been properly included in the trust. We verify this by checking how the tax bill is addressed. We even consult the county assessor's records. Unfortunately, we discover that some attorneys have drafted trust documents without properly funding them. When trusts go unfunded, it renders the trusts ineffective and ultimately a waste of money.

You Can't Take It With You

When it comes to legacy and estate planning strategies, the most important thing is to *do it*. I have heard people from clients to celebrities (rap artist Snoop Dogg comes to mind) say they aren't interested in what happens to their assets when they die because they'll be dead. That's certainly one way to look at it. But I think that's a very selfish way to go about things. We all have people and causes we care about, and those who care about us. Even if the people we love don't *need* what we leave behind, they can still be fined or legally tied up in the probate process or burial costs if we don't plan for those. And that's not even considering what happens if you become incapacitated at some point while you are still alive. Having a plan in place can greatly reduce the stress of those responsibilities on your loved ones; it's just a loving thing to do.

Documents

There are a few documents that lay the groundwork for legacy planning. You've probably heard of all or most of them, but I'd like to review what they are and how people commonly use them. These are all things you should talk about with an estate planning attorney to establish your legacy.

Powers of Attorney

A power of attorney, or POA, is a document giving someone the authority to act on your behalf and in your best interests. These come in handy in situations where you cannot be present (think of a vacation where you get stuck in Canada), or for durable powers of attorney (DPOA), even when you are incapacitated (think in a coma or coping with dementia).

It is important to have powers of attorney in place and to appoint someone you trust to act on your behalf in these matters. Have you ever heard of someone who was incapacitated after a car accident, whether from head trauma or being in a coma for weeks — sometimes months? Do you think their bills stopped coming due during that time? I like my phone company and my bank, but neither one is about to put a moratorium on sending me bills — particularly not for an extended or interminable period. A power of attorney would have the authority to pay your mortgage or cancel your cable while you are unable.

You can have multiple attorneys-in-fact and require them to act jointly.

What this looks like: Do you think two heads are better than one? One man, Chris, significantly relied on his two sons' opinions for both his business and personal matters. He appointed both sons as attorneys-in-fact, requiring both their signoffs for his medical and financial matters.

You can have multiple attorneys-in-fact who can act independently.

What this looks like: Irene had three children with whom she routinely stayed. They lived in different areas of the country, which she thought was an advantage; one month she might be hiking out West, the next she could enjoy the newest off-Broadway production, and the next she could soak up some Southern sun. She named her three children as independently authorized attorneys-in-fact, so if something happened, no matter where she was, the child closest could step in to act on her behalf.

You can have attorneys-in-fact who have different responsibilities.

What this looks like: Although Luke's friend Claire, a nurse, was his go-to and attorney-in-fact for health-related issues, financial matters usually made her nervous, so he appointed his good neighbor, Matt, as his attorney-in-fact in all of his financial and legal matters.

In addition to POAs, it may be helpful to have an advanced health care directive (HCD), which is sometimes referenced as a **living will.** This is a document where you have pre-decided what choices you would make about different health scenarios.

An advanced health care directive can help ease the burden for your medical attorney-in-fact and loved ones, particularly when it comes to end-of-life care.

Do you know that the loved ones of a prominent chief justice of the Supreme Court once had to go through the public agony of probate? Warren Burger typed his own will prior to his death, but it contained just 176 words and was considered by critics to have inadequately addressed matters pertaining to his estate.[63]

His property had to go through probate, which can become a crucial issue when it comes to wills, as it sometimes validates their authenticity. This is why estates left by famous celebrities such as Prince often face challenges, with various individuals claiming that they were intended to be beneficiaries.

To circumvent such situations, creating a trust instead of solely relying on a will can be a wise decision. A trust, when properly executed, eliminates the potential for disputes over the estate.

Recognize, too, that it is vital to ensure that your POA is durable. This means that it remains valid even if you become mentally incapacitated, avoiding any nullification.

Wills

Perhaps the most basic document of legacy planning, a will is a legal document wherein you outline your wishes for your estate. When it comes to your estate after your death, having a will is the foundation of your legacy. Without one, your loved ones are left behind to guess what you would have wanted, and the court will likely split your assets according to the state's probate laws. As far as anyone knows, maybe that's exactly what you wanted, right? Because even if you told your nephew he could have your

---

[63] The Washington Post. 1995. "Former Chief Justice Burger Leaves Heirs Exposed to Tax"
https://www.washingtonpost.com/archive/politics/1995/11/01/former-chief-justice-burger-leaves-heirs-exposed-to-tax/31f4d85f-e0cc-41d5-b459-cd80cc27b3b7/

car he's been driving, if it's not in writing, it still might go to the brother, sister, son, or daughter to whom you aren't speaking.

However, it may not be enough just to have a will. Even with a will, your assets will be subject to probate. Probate is what we call the state's process for determining a will's validity. A judge will go through your will to question if it conflicts with state law, if it is the most up-to-date document, if you were mentally competent at the time it was in order, etc. For some, this is a quick, easily resolved process. For others, particularly if someone steps forward to contest the will, it may take years to settle, all the while subjecting the assets to court costs and attorney's fees.

One other undesirable piece of the probate process is that it is a public process. That means anyone can go to the courthouse, ask for copies of the case, and discover your assets. They can also see who is slated to receive what and who is disputing.

Imagine this scenario: You're walking down the street when someone approaches you and asks, "How much money do you have?" Naturally, you'd be taken aback and consider it none of their business.

However, in the unfortunate event of your passing, anyone can go to the courthouse and find out exactly how much money you have if your estate planning requires the use of the probate process. Suppose you have a secret, something you've kept hidden from everyone — perhaps a child born out of wedlock or with a mistress. You've been providing financial support for the child discreetly all these years, and you want to continue caring for them even after you're gone.

By simply letting your estate go through probate and including them in your will, everyone will learn about the child. However, with proper estate planning, you can ensure that this sensitive information remains private, unknown to the world. So, remember, probate is a public process, and it can be quite time-consuming — and costly.

To probate an estate commonly costs around 5 percent of the estate's value.[64] Consider this: for a $1 million estate, you could be looking at a hefty $50,000 in attorney fees just for the probate process. Suppose you have no significant funds, except for a $1 million house. If this house isn't properly arranged to pass on to your heirs as you wish, or even if it's arranged through a will that needs to go through probate, guess what?

An attorney could charge $50,000 to navigate the probate process. But here's an alternative: instead of enduring all that hassle, in Missouri and many other states you could have chosen a simple one- or two-page beneficiary deed. This solution would have only cost you around $200, plus filing fees at the courthouse, to ensure that your property is transferred smoothly to your children.

It's also important to remember beneficiary designations trump wills. So, that large life insurance policy? What if, when you bought it fifteen years ago, you wrote your ex-husband's name on the beneficiary line? Even if you stipulate otherwise in your will, the company that holds your policy will pay out to your ex-spouse. Or how about the thousands of dollars in your IRA you dedicated to the children thirty years ago, but one of your children was killed in a car accident, leaving his wife and two toddlers behind? That IRA may transfer to your remaining children, effectively disinheriting the grandchildren born to your deceased child.

That may paint a grim portrait, but I can't underscore enough the importance of working with a skilled estate planning attorney to keep your will and beneficiary designations up to date as your life changes.

I once heard about a gentleman named Dave, who dedicated his entire career to one company. He diligently set up his 401(k) plan through his employer, designating his wife as the

---

[64] True Tamplin. Finance Stategists. September 7, 2023. "Standard Probate Fees" https://www.financestrategists.com/estate-planning-lawyer/probate/standard-probate-fees/

beneficiary. Unfortunately, life took its toll, and the couple went through a difficult divorce.

Dave moved on and found happiness with another woman, whom he married. They were together for more than thirty years. Dave and his second wife each assumed that the money in Dave's 401(k) would naturally go to his current wife.

Unfortunately, Dave never updated his beneficiary designation form. Shockingly, his ex-wife from roughly forty years earlier was still listed as the beneficiary. As hard as it may be to believe, the woman he barely knew and had long since parted ways with would receive all the savings in his 401(k), which amounted to roughly $1 million.

This unfortunate situation teaches us a valuable lesson. What and who gets listed on a beneficiary designation form outweighs anything stated in your will, trust, or other documents. That beneficiary designation holds all the power. It's crucial to regularly review and update your retirement accounts, especially where beneficiaries are concerned.

A financial advisor should conduct a beneficiary audit every year during your financial planning sessions. They'll make sure all your accounts reflect your current wishes, and they'll make any necessary changes. If your advisor neglects this vital step, it's time to question whether they truly have your best interests at heart.

Remember, keeping your beneficiaries up-to-date is not something to take lightly. The future financial security of your loved ones may depend on it.

Trusts

Another piece of legacy planning to consider are trusts. A trust is set up through an attorney who appoints and authorizes a trusted party or trustee(s) to administer the trust (e.g., make decisions, manage the assets in the trust, distribute funds from the trust, etc.) according to the provisions of the trust agreement.

Many people are skeptical of trusts because they assume trusts are only appropriate for the fabulously wealthy. A simple trust will likely cost more than $1,000 if prepared by an estate planning attorney, and fees can be higher for couples.[65] But a trust can help you avoid both the expense and publicity of probate, provide a more immediate transfer of wealth, avoid some taxes, and provide you greater control over your legacy.

For instance, if you want to set aside some funds for a grandchild's college education, you can make it a requirement that they enroll in classes before your trust will dispense any funds. Like a will, beneficiary designations will override your trust conditions, so you still should be keeping your beneficiary designations on insurance policies, investment accounts (e.g., 401(k)s, IRAs), and other assets up to date.

Like any financial or legal consideration, there are many options these days beyond the simple "yes or no" question of whether to have a trust. For one thing, you will need to consider if you want your trust to be revocable (you can change the terms while you are alive) or irrevocable (can't be changed; you are no longer the "owner" of the contents).

A brief note here about irrevocable trusts: Although they have significant and greater tax benefits, they are still subject to a Medicaid look-back period. If you transfer your assets into an irrevocable trust in an attempt to shelter them from a Medicaid spend-down, you will be ineligible for Medicaid coverage of long-term care for five years. However, an irrevocable trust can avoid both probate and estate taxes, and it can even help protect assets from legal judgments against you.

Another thing to remember when it comes to trusts, in general, is that even if you have set up a trust, you must remember to fund it. In my thirty-one years' work, I've had numerous clients come to me assuming they have helped

---

[65] Rickie Houston. SmartAsset. April 5, 2023. "How Much Does It Cost to Set Up a Trust? https://smartasset.com/estate-planning/how-much-does-it-cost-to-set-up-a-trust

protect their assets with a trust. When we talk about taxes and other pieces of their legacy, it turns out they never retitled any assets or changed any paperwork on the assets they wanted in the trust. So, please remember, a trust is just a bunch of fancy legal papers if you haven't followed through on retitling your assets.

We take the responsibility of helping clients understand and leverage their assets seriously. By properly utilizing trust structures, we can ensure that clients' wishes are carried out seamlessly. Let's delve into a few scenarios to illustrate the importance of trusts.

Suppose you have children from different marriages. In such cases, a trust can provide a practical solution to ensure your assets go to your intended beneficiaries. However, if you have two children from a marriage and explicitly want the money to go directly to them, setting up a trust may not be necessary. Assessing the stability of their relationships and their maturity can guide us in finding a more straightforward approach.

Another situation where a trust becomes invaluable is when you have a grandchild with unique care needs. By setting aside a dedicated sum of money solely for their benefit, you can secure their future.

In your family, you may find that one child has achieved great success, enjoying financial abundance. On the other hand, another child may have faced numerous challenges, with a difficult journey, a less financially rewarding career, and additional burdens in their personal life. Their children may struggle academically, and their spouse may not provide the necessary support.

When it comes to dividing your assets, it may not be best to split everything equally. Remember, there is nothing more unequal than the equal treatment of unequals. It is perfectly acceptable to provide more or less support to each child based on their individual needs.

Our objective is to guide you through the estate planning process and determine the most suitable solutions tailored to your specific circumstances. It's not just about trusts, or any other estate planning instruments. It's about making informed decisions to safeguard your legacy.

Taxes

Although charitable contributions, trusts, and other tax-efficient strategies can reduce your tax bill, it's unlikely your estate will be passed on entirely tax-free. Yet, when it comes to building a legacy that can last for generations, taxes can be one of the heaviest drains on the impact of your hard work.

For 2024, the federal estate exemption was $13.61 million per individual and $27.22 million for a married couple, with estates facing up to a 40 percent tax rate after that.[66] Currently, the new estate limits are set to increase with inflation until January 1, 2026, when they will "sunset" back to the inflation-adjusted 2017 limits.[67] And that's not taking into account the various state regulations and taxes regarding estate and inheritance transfers.

Another tax concern "frequent flyer": retirement accounts.

Your IRA or 401(k) can be a source of tax issues when you pass away. For one thing, taking funds from a sizeable account can trigger a large tax bill. However, if you leave the assets in the account, there are still required minimum distributions (RMDs), which will take effect even after you die. If you pass the account to your spouse, they can keep taking your RMDs as is, or your spouse can retitle the account in their name and receive RMDs based on their life expectancy. Remember, if you don't take your RMDs, the IRS will take up to 25 percent of your required distribution (10 percent if corrections are made in a timely fashion). You will still have to pay income taxes whenever you withdraw that money. Provisions in the original

---

[66] Katelyn Washington. Kiplinger. November 15, 2023. "What's the 2024 Estate Tax Exemption?" https://www.kiplinger.com/taxes/estate-tax-exemption-amount-increases
[67] Internal Revenue Service. November 22, 2023. "What's New - Estate and Gift Tax" https://www.irs.gov/businesses/small-businesses-self-employed/whats-new-estate-and-gift-tax

SECURE Act require anyone who inherits your IRA, with few exceptions (your spouse, a beneficiary less than ten years younger, or a disabled adult child, to name a few), to empty the account within ten years of your death.

Also — and this is a pretty big also — check with an estate planning attorney if you are considering putting your IRA or 401(k) in a trust. An improperly titled beneficiary form for the IRA could mean the difference of thousands of dollars in taxes. This is just one more reason to work with a financial professional, one who can strategically partner with an estate planning attorney and also, a tax advisor, to diligently check your decisions.

CHAPTER 9

Women Retire Too

I help women, and families from all walks of life on their journey to and through retirement. However, we want to address the female demographic specifically. Why? To be perfectly blunt, women are more likely to deal with poverty than men when they reach retirement.

The overall poverty rate for women slightly exceeds the rate for men, but among those seventy-five years and older, 13.51 percent of women live at the poverty rate compared to 8.82 percent of men.[68]

The topics, products, and strategies I cover elsewhere in this book are meant to help address retirement concerns for men *and* women, but the dire statistic above is a reminder that much of traditional planning is geared toward men. Male careers, male lifespans, male health care. The bottom line is women's career paths often look much different than men's, so why would their retirement planning look the same?

Women often embrace different roles and values than men as workers, wives, mothers, and daughters. They are more apt to take on roles as caretakers, thus women are likely to spend portions of their lives making hard shifts between family and careers. Time out of the workforce means less income accumulation for investments and retirement. Also, non-

---

[68] Statista. September 22, 2022. "Poverty rate in the United States in 2021, by age and gender" https://www.statista.com/statistics/233154/us-poverty-rate-by-gender/

working years count as zeroes when calculating Social Security benefits. Women who strongly value family and community tend to focus on lifetime gifting and legacy funding, sometimes to the detriment of their own lifestyles.

These unique choices, challenges, and hurdles make a solid case that women deserve special consideration from financial professionals. The argument is further promoted by the fact that 69 percent of men in the U.S. age sixty-five and older happen to be married, compared to 47 percent of women in that age classification.[69] Single women don't have the opportunity to capitalize on the resource pooling and potential economies of scale accompanying a marriage or partnership.

When couples embark on the financial planning process, it's crucial to address the potential future. One thing to consider is that eventually, there may be only one person remaining at the table. It's important to ensure that provisions are in place to support that individual.

Some key insights to keep in mind:
- When one spouse passes away, the surviving spouse often faces a higher tax bracket. Taxes are structured to provide benefits for married couples, so being widowed could result in increased tax payments compared to when both spouses were alive. It's essential to plan for this potential change and its financial implications, which may include higher Medicare costs.
- In many cases, it is the woman who outlives her spouse. We often see husbands bringing their wives to us without explicitly stating that, as men, they are concerned about their own longevity. They entrust us to take care of their loved ones. It's crucial to acknowledge this underlying message and address it openly. We need to analyze the impact of long-term care on income,

---

[69] Administration for Community Living. November 30, 2022. "Profile of Older Americans" https://acl.gov/aging-and-disability-in-america/data-and-research/profile-older-americans

lifestyle, and potential depletion of savings for both partners.
- It's also essential to evaluate the consequences of premature death for either spouse. How would it affect income, lifestyle, and financial sustainability? We must conduct an in-depth analysis to understand the potential tax implications when one of you passes away.

By openly recognizing and discussing these possibilities, we gently guide couples to face the music and proactively tackle these eventual issues. It's crucial to plan ahead, as these situations will inevitably become a reality for every family.

Be Informed

With all the couples I've seen, there is almost always an "alpha" when it comes to finances. It isn't always men. For many of my coupled clients, the wife is the alpha who keeps the books and budgets and knows where all of the family's assets are, down to the penny. Yet, statistically, among baby boomers, it is usually a man who runs the books. But as time goes on, it looks like the ratio of male to female financial alphas is evening out, based on my experience speaking with couples.

Because most of the baby boomer alphas are men, there is an all too familiar scene in many financial offices across the country: A woman comes into an appointment carrying a sack full of unopened envelopes. Often through tears, she sits across the desk from a financial professional and apologizes her way through a conversation about what financial products she owns and where her income is coming from. She is recently widowed and was sure her spouse was taking care of the finances, but now she doesn't know where all their assets are kept, and her confidence in her financial outlook has wavered after walking through funeral expenses and realizing she's down to one income.

Often, she may be financially "okay." Yet, the uncertainty can be wearying, particularly when the family is already reeling from a loss. While this scenario sometimes plays out with men, in my experience, it's more likely to be a woman in that chair across from my desk. Although the practice has been leveling more and more in recent decades, for centuries Western traditions held money management down as being "a guy thing." But it doesn't have to be this way. This all-too-common scenario can be wiped away with just a little preparation.

Talk to Your Spouse/ Work with a Financial Professional

While there are many factors affecting women's financial preparation for and situation in retirement, I cannot emphasize enough that the decision to be informed, to be a part of the conversation, and to be aware of what is going on with your finances is absolutely paramount to a confident retirement.

The breakdown regarding couples and finances seems to happen because of a lack of communication The breakdown often seems to stem from no one other than the financial alpha knowing how much the family has and where. In the end, it doesn't matter who handles the money; it's about all parties being informed of what's going on financially.

There are a lot of ways to open the conversation about money. One woman, Ann, started a conversation with her husband, the financial alpha, by sitting down and saying, "Teach me how to be a widow." Perhaps that sounds grim, but it was to the point, and it spurred what she said was a very fruitful conversation. Couples sometimes have their first real conversation about money, assets, and their retirement income approach in our office. The important thing about having these conversations isn't where; it's when. The best "when" is as soon as possible.

Ann told me that after they got the conversation rolling, she and her husband spent a day — just one part of an otherwise dull weekend — going through everything she might need to know. They spent the better part of two decades together after that. When he died and she was widowed, she said the "widowhood" talk had made a huge difference. She knew who to call to talk through their retirement plan and where to call for the insurance policy.

She said the benefit of the weekend exercise they engaged in some twenty years earlier couldn't have been more apparent than when she ultimately accompanied a recently widowed friend to a financial appointment. Her friend was emotional the whole time, afraid she would run out of money any day. The financial professional ultimately showed the friend that she was financially in good shape, but not before the friend had already spent months worried that each check would exhaust her bank account. That's no way to live after losing a loved one. It was preventable had her deceased spouse and financial professional included her in a conversation about "widowhood."

Spouse-Specific Options

One area where it might be especially important to be on the same page between spouses is when it comes to financial products or services that have spousal options. A few that come to mind are pensions and Social Security, although life insurance and annuity policies also have the potential to affect both spouses.

With pensions, taking the worker's life-only option is somewhat attractive. After all, the monthly payment is bigger. However, you and your spouse should discuss your options. When we're talking about both of you as opposed to just one lifespan, there is an increased likelihood that at least one of you will live a long, long time. This means the monthly payout will be less, but it also helps ensure that no matter which spouse outlives the other, no one will have to suffer the loss of a needed pension paycheck in their later retirement years.

While we covered Social Security options in a different chapter, I think some of the spousal information bears repeating. Particularly, if you worked exclusively inside the home for a significant number of years, you may want to talk about taking your Social Security benefits based on your spouse's work history. After all, Social Security is based on your thirty-five highest-earning years.

Things to remember about the spousal benefits:[70]
- Your benefit will be calculated as a percentage (up to 50 percent) of your spouse's earned monthly benefit at their full retirement age (or FRA).
- For you to begin receiving a spousal benefit, your spouse must have already filed for their benefits, and you must be at least sixty-two.
- You can qualify for a full half of your spouse's benefits if you wait until you reach FRA to file.
- Beginning your benefits earlier than your FRA will reduce your monthly check, but waiting to file until after FRA will not increase your benefits.

For divorcees:[71]
- You may qualify for an ex-spousal benefit if …
  a. You were married for a decade or more
  b. *and* you are at least sixty-two
  c. *and* you have been divorced for at least two years
  d. *and* you are currently unmarried
  e. *and* your ex-spouse is sixty-two (qualifies to begin taking Social Security)
- Your ex-spouse does not need to have filed for you to file on their benefit.
- Similar to spousal benefits, you can qualify for up to half of your ex-spouse's benefits if you wait to file until your FRA.
- If your ex-spouse dies, you may file to receive a widow/widower benefit on their Social Security record as long as you are at least age sixty and fulfill all the other requirements on the preceding alphabetized list.

---

[70] Social Security Administration. 2024. "Benefits For Your Family" https://www.ssa.gov/benefits/retirement/planner/applying7.html
[71] Ibid.

a. This will not affect the benefits of your ex-spouse's current spouse

For widow's (or widower's, for that matter) benefits:[72]
- You may qualify to receive as much as your deceased spouse would have received if ...
    a. You were married for at least nine months before their death
    b. *or* you would qualify for a divorced spousal benefit (if you were divorced and your ex-spouse dies)
    c. *and* you are at least sixty
    d. *and* you did not/have not remarried before age sixty
- You may earn delayed credits on your spouse's benefit *if* your spouse hadn't already filed for benefits when they died.
- Other rules may apply to you if you are disabled or are caring for a deceased spouse's dependent or disabled child.

Longevity

On average, women live longer than men. Most stats put average female longevity at about two years more than men. But averages are tricky things. An April 2022 report by the World Economic Forum listed the eight oldest people in the world as all being women. They ranged in age from 114 years old to 118 and included two Americans.[73]

---

[72] Social Security Administration. 2024. "If You Are the Survivor" https://www.ssa.gov/benefits/survivors/ifyou.html
[73] Martin Armstrong. World Economic Forum. April 29, 2022. "How old are the world's oldest people?" https://www.weforum.org/agenda/2022/04/the-oldest-people-in-the-world/

It's an exciting time to be a woman, as their potential life paths are vast and less subject to judgment than probably at any point in history. Want to stay at home and raise children? Wonderful! Get a PhD in Astrophysics and work for NASA? Fantastic! Do a combination of both? It's happening! On one hand, women all have unique personalities, goals, ambitions, and passions. However, they share biological and instinctual traits that, in general, give rise to longer lives. And, on that note, the trend for women to live longer presents longstanding financial ramifications.

Statistics on longevity show that women often outlive their husbands, sometimes by a significant margin. This can result in a period of two decades or more where women are on their own. It's crucial to plan accordingly.

While I hope to live a long and healthy life myself, I am aware of genetic factors that may affect my lifespan. My paternal grandfather died at sixty-five and was survived by my grandmother, who lived to eighty-six. My maternal grandfather died at seventy-two and was survived by my grandmother, who lived to ninety-four. While I hope to live a long time, I understand my genetic makeup.

Meanwhile, my wife is a lean, exercising machine who maintains a balanced diet and leads an active lifestyle. With her dedication to wellness, it's possible that she could live to be 110 years old.

Generally, our clients' retirement plans are designed to provide income until age 100. However, in my wife's case, I want to ensure that she is financially secure until age 110. I wouldn't want to leave her in her later years without any financial support.

Of course, we have to be realistic and set reasonable expectations, considering that there are limits to how long we should map out a retirement income plan. But when I observe the trend of increasing life expectancy, especially with advancements in medicine and growing awareness of health, I believe that my daughters, who are currently in their mid-20s, have a good chance of living to 100 or beyond. These changes necessitate adaptation and preparation for longer lifespans.

In general, it's safe to assume that most wives will outlive their husbands. It is essential to keep this in mind when planning for the future.

Simply Needing More Money in Retirement

Living longer in retirement means needing more money. Period. Barring a huge lottery win or some crazy stock market action, the date you retire is likely the point at which you have the most money you will ever have. Not to put too grim a spin on it, but the problem with longevity is the further you get away from that date, the further your dollars have to stretch. If you only planned to live to a nice eighty-something but instead live to a nice 100-something, that is *two decades* you will need to account for monetarily.

To put this in perspective, let's say you like to drink coffee as an everyday splurge. Not accounting for inflation or leap years, a $4 cup-a-day habit is $29,200 over a two-decade span. Now, think of all the things you like to do that cost money. Add those up for twenty years of unanticipated costs. I think you'll see what I mean.

More Health Care Needs

In addition to the cost of living for a longer lifespan is the fact that aging — plain and simple — means more health care, and more health care means more money. Women are survivors. They suffer from the morbidity-mortality paradox, which states women suffer more non-fatal illnesses throughout their lifetime than men, who experience fewer illnesses but higher mortality.

Women have been found to seek treatment more often when not feeling well and emphasize staying healthy when older, according to studies. Survival, I believe, is on the side of the woman. However, surviving things (such as cancer) also means more checkups later in life.

A statistical concern for women involves the prospect of long-term care. Long-term care for women lasts 3.7 years on average compared to 2.2 years for men.[74]

Widowhood

Not only do women typically live longer than their same-age male counterparts, but they also stand a greater chance of living alone as they age. Some divorce, separate, or never marry. Among those age sixty-five and over, 33 percent of women live alone compared to 20 percent of men.[75]

I don't write this to scare people; rather, I think it's fundamentally important to prepare my female clients for something that may be a startling *but very likely* scenario. At some point, most women will have to handle their financial situations on their own. A little preparation can go a long way, and having a basic understanding of your household finances and the "who, what, where, and how much" of your family's assets is incredibly useful. It can prevent a tragic situation from being more traumatic.

In my opinion, the financial services industry sometimes underserves women in these situations. Some financial professionals tend to alienate women, even when their spouses are alive. I've heard several stories of women who sat through meeting after meeting without their financial professional ever addressing a single question to them.

In our firm, when we work with couples, we work hard to make sure our retirement income strategies work for *both*

---

[74] Lindsay Modglin. SingleCare. January 24, 2024. "Long-term care statistics 2024" https://www.singlecare.com/blog/news/long-term-care-statistics/

[75] Statista. November 23, 2022. "Share of senior households living alone in the United States 2020, by gender" https://www.statista.com/statistics/912400/senior-households-living-alone-usa/

people. No matter who the financial alpha is, it's important for everyone affected by a retirement strategy to understand it.

When faced with loss and uncertainty, the first step is to pause and find stillness. It may take time, even years, to regain your balance and adjust to not having your spouse by your side. It's a challenge I can empathize with, and my heart goes out to those in such a situation.

A sense of calm in a time of grief can be soothing. Again, that's why I tell my clients not to rush into anything under such circumstances.

Granted, there are necessary steps to take, such as notifying Social Security and making life insurance claims, but refrain from making drastic changes to your life. If we've done our job well, your retirement plan is already designed to ensure a smooth transition for both of you as a couple and, eventually, one of you alone.

Taxes

One of the often-unexpected aspects of widowhood is the tax bill. Many women continue similar lifestyles to the ones they shared with their spouses. This, in turn, means continuing to have a similar need for income. However, after the death of a spouse, their taxes will be calculated based on a single filer's income table, which is much less forgiving than the couple's tax rates. With proper planning, your financial professional and tax advisor may be able to help you take the sting out of your new tax status.

Caregiving

In addition to the financial burden created by caregiving responsibilities, many women often devote many hours each day to duties such as housekeeping and looking after loved ones. So then, when can women find the time to focus long and hard on financial matters?

Unfortunately, the impact and hardships created by traditional roles for women typically do not account for Social Security benefit losses or the losses of health care benefits and retirement savings. This also doesn't account for maternity care, mothers who homeschool, or women who leave the workforce to care for their children in any way.

I don't repeat these statistics to scare you. In America, about 53 million serve as unpaid caregivers and spend roughly $7,000 annually on out-of-pocket caregiving costs.[76] Yet, I think the emotional value of the care many women provide their elderly relatives or neighbors cannot be quantified. So, to be clear, this shouldn't be taken as a "why not to provide caregiving" spiel. Instead, it should be seen as a call for "why to *prepare* for caregiving" or "how to lessen the financial and emotional burden of caregiving."

Funding Your Own Retirement

For these reasons, women should be prepared to fund more of their own retirements. There are several savings options and products, including the spousal IRA. They are like a typical IRA except used by a person who's married. The working spouse must earn at least as much money as is contributed into the IRA.[77] This is something to consider, particularly for families where one spouse has dropped out of the workforce to care for a relative. Also, if you find yourself in a caregiving role, talk to your employer's human resources department. Some companies have paid leave, special circumstances, or sick leave options you could qualify for, making it easier to cope and helping you stay longer in the workforce.

---

[76] The Scan Foundation. November 10, 2022. "Family caregivers are unsung heroes" https://www.thescanfoundation.org/the-buzz/family-caregivers-are-unsung-heroes.

[77] Andrea Coombes. NerdWallet. November 2, 2023. "Spousal IRA: What It Is, How to Open One"
https://www.nerdwallet.com/article/investing/spousal-ira-what-it-is-and-why-you-should-open-one

Saving Money

Women likely need more money to fund their retirements. But this doesn't have to be a significant burden. Often, women are better at saving, while usually taking less risk in their portfolios. One source identified many ways in which women are crushing this retirement component.[78]

- In a 2021 analysis of five million Fidelity customers over a ten-year period, women's investment rates of return outperformed men by .04 percent.
- Wells Fargo found that women take approximately 82 percent of the risk men take.
- Meghan Railey, co-founder and CEO of Optas Capital, wrote, "While we have found that male clients tend to eagerly invest in the latest asset class everyone is talking about, like cryptocurrency, female clients do not generally jump on the shiny bandwagon."
- Women do a better job buying and holding quality stocks and avoid impulsive decisions. Staying invested for the long haul is often cited as the most effective investing strategy.
- Women remain calm and are less likely to liquidate their retirement accounts during market volatility.
- Lastly, Vanguard found women are less active investors, logging on to their accounts half as often as men and trading 40 percent less frequently.

With all the hurdles to retirement that are unique to women, it's exciting they inherently have an advantage when it comes to saving. This gives me reason to believe as women get more involved in their finances, families will continue to become more confident about retirement.

---

[78] Lyle Daly. The Motley Fool. February 20, 2024. "Investing for Women: What You Should Know"
https://www.fool.com/research/women-in-investing-research/

CHAPTER 10

Long-Term Care

Elsewhere in this book, I've outlined the risks longevity poses to your financial health. In fact, you may be tired of reading it at this point.

Even so, I'd still like to repeat one more time — in case you've forgotten — it's estimated *seven* out of every ten Americans who reach age sixty-five will need long-term care of some kind.[79] Let me ask: If you knew the car you were going to be riding in had a 70 percent chance of having an accident, would you wear your seatbelt?

When we discuss long-term care, what immediately comes to mind? Most often, it's a nursing home. However, long-term care encompasses much more than that. It can also involve care within the comfort of your own home. It could mean having someone by your side to assist with everyday tasks like getting out of bed, bathing, dressing, cooking meals, administering medication, or even running errands and doing your shopping.

Long-term care can include adult day care or assisted living. So when we mention "long-term care," we aren't assuming that everyone will spend time in a nursing home. However, it's highly probable that at some point in your life, you will require some form of care.

---

[79] Lindsay Modglin. SingleCare. January 24, 2024. "Long-term care statistics 2024" https://www.singlecare.com/blog/news/long-term-care-statistics/

These issues surrounding the prospect of long-term care are primary catalysts for bringing individuals through our doors. They are perturbed and disheartened by the complex nature of long-term care. The bottom line is we must plan for the possibility of long-term care. If you think about the current problems plaguing government-run programs such as Social Security, Medicaid, and Medicare, I think it stands to reason we're probably on our own for planning how to pay for this.

Five Ways to Pay for Long-Term Care

Let's explore methods for covering long-term care costs:

Self-insurance: This means paying for long-term care out of your own pocket. Have you ever wondered how much a one-year stay in a long-term care facility costs in southwest Missouri? On average, it's around $84,000 per year. Imagine that cost multiplied by three years for men, which amounts to roughly $252,000. For women, who tend to live longer, the average stay could be as much as five years, costing around $420,000. And don't forget about inflation and how it could impact costs moving forward.

Irrevocable Trust: This method involves transferring all your assets into a trust that you no longer control. By doing so, you are considered financially destitute and can qualify for Medicaid. However, most people prefer not to rely on Medicaid if there's another viable option.

Annuity: One of the solutions you may consider is an annuity — a financial tool that many of us will likely possess in the future. Think about what I wrote previously. Do you currently receive or anticipate receiving Social Security? Or, perhaps you have a pension lined up? Well, guess what? Congratulations! You already have an annuity.

Simply put, an annuity guarantees a steady and reliable stream of income throughout your lifetime. It's designed to provide financial security. Now, let's say you find yourself in a situation where your Social Security and pension income might not be sufficient. Well, you can opt to transfer a lump sum to an insurance company and secure a future annuity check to cover long-term care expenses when the time comes.

Long-Term Care Insurance: Imagine having a folder in your hands, containing a free long-term care insurance policy that would secure you and your spouse for a lifetime. It would be a hassle-free way to cover an inevitable cost. Wouldn't you ensure that folder reaches home with you? The truth is, most of us desire this coverage, but hesitate when it comes to paying for it. One factor that holds us back is the "use it or lose it" component. If you never require long-term care and pass away peacefully in your sleep (wouldn't that be ideal?), your insurance becomes null and void. It's comparable to paying for fire insurance and never experiencing a house fire. It feels like a gamble.

Take a moment to look at towering skyscrapers in a big city. What names do you see at the very top? Quite often, it's prominent insurance companies. I always figure those buildings are paid for by people who had long-term care insurance, and died in their sleep, never using it.

Another long-term care insurance predicament often arises. Year after year, insureds receive letters notifying them of increased premiums or reduced benefits. It leaves them with a mere thirty days to make a tough decision. Exploring the numbers reveals a policy that's either worthless or priced so high that it's ultimately unsustainable. That's why long-term care insurance is no longer a viable option.

Life Insurance with Accelerated Death Benefit: With properly structured life insurance, the accelerated death benefit (ADB) is tax-free, ensuring your family receives the full amount after your passing. An ADB allows you to access a portion of the death benefit while you're alive, providing funds for long-term care expenses.

Suppose you have a $100,000 death benefit and require long-term care. The insurance company will advance the death benefit to cover your care expenses. If, after one year, you spent

$80,000 on care, your spouse would still receive the remaining $20,000 tax-free.

The appeal of life insurance with an ADB lies in the ability to reclaim your investment without any loss. Premiums can be fixed and the death benefit guaranteed, offering peace of mind. Considering these advantages, life insurance with an ADB can be an appealing option for financing your long-term care needs.

Long-Term Care Solutions: It's Not Just About You

One of the most compelling arguments in favor of preparing for the likelihood of long-term care has less to do with our own personal assets and more to do with others.

What do I mean? Well, I hear from lots of people who think it won't matter. "Oh, by the time I reach the point of needing long-term care, I'll be out of my mind. Who cares who takes care of me and how that happens?"

However, like estate planning, long-term care planning isn't solely about us. In fact, I might argue that the most important piece of long-term care planning isn't about you at all. It's about your loved ones. It's about your spouse, your children, or your friends, and how caring for you could impact them if you don't have the necessary resources.

Most caregiving for the elderly happens in people's private homes. A survey of caregivers reveals just a sampling of how a long stint of caring for relatives and loved ones can affect caregivers:[80]

- Of those surveyed, a mean of nineteen hours a week was provided in care. Among those, about 38 percent had to cut back their hours at their job.

---

[80] Genworth. November 16, 2021. "Beyond Dollars 2021" https://pro.genworth.com/riiproweb/productinfo/pdf/682801BRO.pdf

- More than half reported that their personal and mental health was impacted, including depression and a lower standard of living.
- Sixty-six percent of caregivers used their personal assets, like savings and retirement funds, to pay for a loved one's care.
- Fifty-two percent of caregivers moved closer to the loved one for whom they provided care.

An In-Home Exercise to Consider

The potential for confronting long-term care expenses is not an absolute plea to rush out and buy a life insurance policy. However, I would strongly suggest putting a long-term care plan in place. If you don't have a plan, the government has one for you. It's called Medicaid, and you'll have to spend down your assets to about $2,000 to qualify.

In some cases, you could be assigned to a Medicaid-only facility. You should think about whether that is where you want to spend your last days.

Who usually gets sick first? The husband. Without proper planning, his illness could cause a family to spend down everything it has saved, leaving his wife with few assets. Consequently, men need to stop rubbing their bellies and pointing to their wives when asked about their long-term care plans. A spouse is not a plan, and if you happen to think your wife is solely responsible for your care, I've got an in-home exercise for you both.

Men: lay down on the bathroom floor. Call for your wife and have her come into the bathroom. Women: Take a look at your husband lying there, then bend down, scoop him up in your arms, carry him into the bedroom, and gently lay him on the bed.

If you can do that, you probably don't need long-term care protection. But the rest of us better get a plan.

Heavenly Ambitions

One evening, my wife Kelly and I had tended to the livestock in our barn and hopped on our John Deere Gator to return to the house. As we drove the quarter-mile or so and got closer, Kelly looked inside the house at the glow inside our fireplace.

"Boy, it sure looks warm in there," Kelly remarked before we pulled around and parked in the garage. "You know, it would be okay to me if Heaven was just like our house."

Kelly is great. She's full of spirit while leading an active lifestyle that includes an unwavering commitment to friends and family, including our adult daughters, Madison and Sydnie. I love them all dearly.

But as we jumped off the Gator that night, after Kelly expressed her satisfaction with the life we've built, I couldn't help but contradict her. "But heaven's not going to be our house," I responded. "Our house pales in comparison to heaven. So imagine how good Heaven will be and what you have to look forward to."

That's how Kelly and I live our lives now. We're not in any hurry to get to Heaven. There's a lot we want to do here, a lot of life we want to live, and a lot of time we still want to spend with our family. But if the news comes that the end is near, and we have to walk that journey that all of us will take someday, Kelly and I are confident in the work Jesus Christ did for us on the cross, paying for our sins to reconcile us with God.

When God looks at us today, he sees us through the lens of Jesus and finds the righteousness of Jesus draped around our shoulders. Not because of our good deeds. We're sinners. But the whole message of Christmas and Easter is wrapped around God sending his son, Jesus, to die in our place, paying the price for our sins. Consequently, we can approach our death with a tremendous sense of confidence. It's going to be okay.

If you receive word that I passed away, don't worry about me. I'm absolutely better than I have ever been in my life. I want Kelly to be taken care of because she's got a big farm, a lot of livestock, and a business to manage. So, I ask our survivors to take care of Kelly and not worry about Barry.

I think if everyone approached the prospect of death through a spiritual lens, it makes estate planning a fairly simple task. When your life is founded and rooted in truth, you view death as something that's going to happen. You anticipate death with confidence, if not anticipation.

Instead, many people want to delay or even disregard estate planning because of some discomfort in dealing with coming to grips with their mortality. They don't want to talk about death, or consider what happens afterward. They don't have the kind of spiritual foundation that prevents them from being afraid, so they just refuse to talk about it.

During estate planning sessions, I will ask people whether they anticipate an inheritance. Often, they'll squirm just a bit and concede that they have no idea. They've told me something to the effect that their father is in his nineties, and they've never spoken about money.

Frankly, that's a shame for the next generation. My children are in their mid-twenties and know about my assets and how they will be distributed. I don't want to be in my nineties and have them tell somebody they don't know about my estate or what I want to leave them. That is not good stewardship.

You should prepare your loved ones for what they are to receive as an inheritance and perhaps even distribute assets to them while you're still living.

.

CHAPTER 11
Finding a Financial Professional

I've spent my life guiding people toward truth and light. Spiritual truth. Eternal light. And financial truth that hopefully shed light on their retirement.

Like the man in the Bible who built his house on a rock, I want to help my clients build their retirement on a sure foundation, so they can be confident that issues in retirement are addressed and they don't need to spend their days in angst or worry about whether they'll have enough.

At the WealthCare Corporation, our process for helping people step into retirement attempts to eliminate as much uncertainty as possible and eliminate angst as much as possible. We do that through what we call Six Steps to Retirement Confidence.

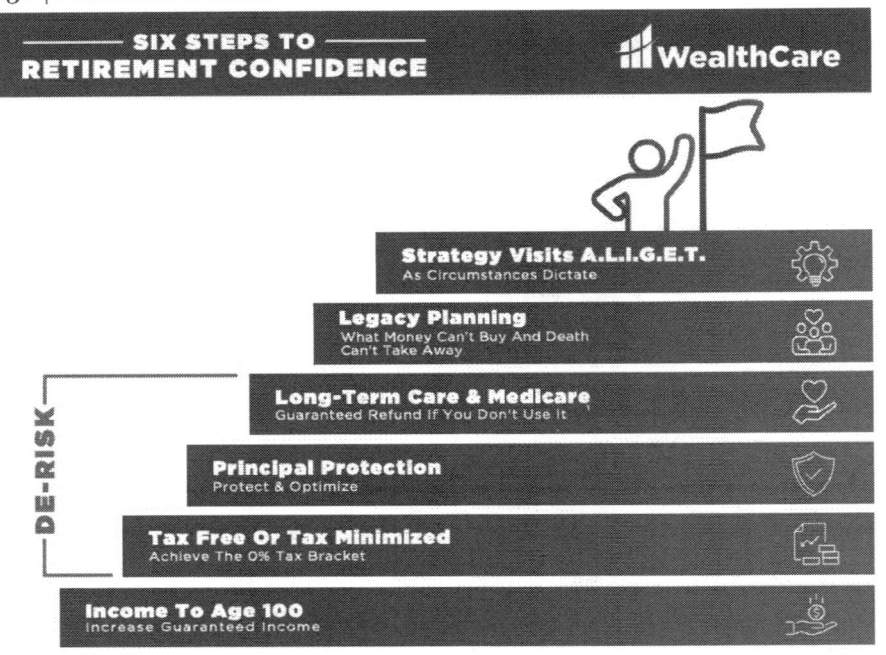

SIX STEPS TO RETIREMENT CONFIDENCE — WealthCare

DE-RISK

- **Strategy Visits A.L.I.G.E.T.** — As Circumstances Dictate
- **Legacy Planning** — What Money Can't Buy And Death Can't Take Away
- **Long-Term Care & Medicare** — Guaranteed Refund If You Don't Use It
- **Principal Protection** — Protect & Optimize
- **Tax Free Or Tax Minimized** — Achieve The 0% Tax Bracket
- **Income To Age 100** — Increase Guaranteed Income

Six Steps to Retirement Confidence

Income to Age 100

Until you know that your income needs are met for each year of retirement, you aren't ready to retire. That's why our retirement planning process starts with Income to Age 100.

We know you might not live to 100. But what if you do? Health care continues to improve. Longevity continues to increase. So, you may live much longer in retirement than you anticipate.

A solid retirement income plan begins by knowing what you want: your "Sittin' on the Porch" number. Then, you must determine what kinds of guaranteed income you have: Social Security, pensions, etc. Now, we can calculate the monthly income that must come from your retirement savings to achieve your lifetime retirement income.

With a high degree of reliability, this allows us to calculate whether you likely have enough money to last throughout retirement or to know when you might run short.

This enables us to make decisions now that might help us extend your money's income span, so you have enough to get through retirement.

Sometimes, we build additional guaranteed income streams through private personal pensions so that you can know exactly what your income will be, guaranteed for all the days of your life.

Tax-Free or Tax-Minimized

Many taxes you pay are actually voluntary. Think of the cartoon caricature of Uncle Sam extending his hand. He could be reaching out and expecting your hard-earned dollars in exchange. But what if you tell him, "Not so fast." Steps exist to reduce or even eliminate certain taxes. Surprisingly, your tax preparer might not discuss these strategies with you.

In our experience, we discovered that approximately one-third of our clients can achieve the zero percent tax bracket either before or very early in retirement. That means they won't pay tax on Social Security and will pay the lowest amount for their Medicare.

Even if you earn $1 million annually, with proper planning, it can all be 100 percent tax-free. Our goal is to help everyone reach the zero percent tax bracket where possible. If that's not possible, we aim to get you into the lowest tax bracket. Why? So that when taxes increase in the future, some say by as much as double, you'd only be back into the 20 percent range. Minimizing or eliminating taxes allows you to take money that would have gone to the IRS or the state government, and redirect it to your retirement income and to your family.

Principal Protection

Everyone has a point at which they can't stand to endure losses any longer. Often, when I speak with a prospective client, I will write the total amount of retirement money they have saved on the board. Then, I'll just draw a line downward to indicate a declining balance from losing money. I'll ask them to stop me when they've lost all they can stand. I've never yet had anyone fail to stop and say, "That's enough."

What's your "enough" number? Generally, that represents the amount of money that someone should set aside in a principal protection program by shifting the risk of loss to the shoulders of a strong financial company.

People do this all the time. You can't afford to lose your home to a tornado or fire, so you shift the risk of that loss to a large financial company. Similarly, you want to be protected from losing your car to an automobile accident, so you shift the risk of that loss to a large financial company. Why should your investment savings be any different?

While many people have retirement savings values that exceed the value of their home, most of them have taken no action to insure those larger assets against loss. I believe that's because they don't know that they can or know how to do it, and in many cases, they just haven't been offered the opportunity. The dread of loss can be buffered. Your income can be protected. Your assets can be insured. Your taxes can be reduced or eliminated. The potentially enormous cost of health care in retirement can be provided for. But to do so, you must use principal protection planning.

Even that portion of your retirement savings that you are willing to have float with the stock market can be buffered against the steep market drops through measures to control volatility.

The point is: You don't have to be a victim to the whims of an ill stock market wind when it blows. You can be protected from loss and buffer yourself from declines if you're open to learning and using new strategies you may not have considered before.

When you discover how to protect yourself from the roller-coaster stock market, it's a step toward retirement confidence.

Long-term Care & Medicine

Not everyone will need long-term care. But how do you know if you will win or lose the long-term care lottery?

Depending on who you listen to, the chances of going into long-term care sometime in your lifetime are somewhere between 70-90 percent. For those that do, the cost is staggering and can destroy the retirement savings you've accumulated. Worse yet, if you are married and go into long-term care, you could spend all the family assets on your care, and then die leaving your surviving spouse without enough retirement income to live, and without the resources to pay for their own long-term care.

If your retirement planner hasn't considered these issues and offered you solutions, that's probably a sign you are receiving guidance from the wrong person. Any planner worth their salt will make sure you've at least had the opportunity to consider your risks, and protect against them to the best of your ability.

Legacy Planning

Estate planning and legacy planning are different. One deals with passing assets to the next generation. One deals with passing closely held values, principles, and truths to grandkids you may never meet.

Which is worth more to you? Financial assets or closely held personal values and truths? Most people think about that and say, "Values and truth." Yet, as a society, we spend billions of dollars writing wills and trusts to pass on the less valuable personal assets. At the same time, we bury the timeless truths and principles in the graveyard with every generation.

I want to change that. That's why I speak of legacy planning instead of estate planning.

Of course, we have to plan to pass your estate on to those you want to receive it. We use wills and trusts to accomplish that. But we use writing and video technology to pass on the real valuable stuff. We guide our clients through a process to record their most private and precious beliefs, and to communicate those to their heirs, so that along with receiving your assets they can also receive your guidance from the grave about what really makes life worth living and about how to remain strong in adversity and overcome the setbacks that life will surely deal them.

Strategy Visits

All five previous steps address what I like to call "boogie men in the bushes." These are the enemies that can derail your retirement. Once you've worked through each of those five steps and eliminated the obstacles, the path in front of you becomes fairly smooth. You just need to watch for any challenges that might resurface.

Approximately once per year, we do a strategy visit with our clients. Whatever we talk about, we make sure that our conversation covers those first five steps again. We want to:

1. Measure your assets. Are they growing? Do you have more than this time last year? Do you need to do anything for yourself or your family because those assets are growing? Do you need to invest in yourself? Improve your home? Do something for your children? Bless a charity? You can't know what you can do, unless you know and measure how your assets are growing.
2. Make sure your income is what you need it to be, enough to meet your needs and wants, but not so much that you're paying unnecessary taxes on it and just re-saving it in a bank account. If needed, we can adjust your income up or down.
3. Make sure you have the cash to do what you want. This is called "liquidity." Often, people who have substantial money feel poor. Somehow, their mind doesn't let them accept that money in their retirement accounts is money that can be spent if they need to, just like money in the bank. We like to calculate liquidity so people know how large of a check they can write, if they want to. Psst. Here's a secret: They

almost never want to. They just want to know they can.
4. Analyze the performance of your investment accounts. We examine how much your accounts have grown or declined in the last year and over the time of our relationship. Are you keeping up with inflation? Do you have the resources you need to do what you want to do? Do you need to rebalance the amounts between protected principal and risk principal, putting growing amounts of risk principal away into safe accounts when it is growing. Or, when the markets fall, taking safe money and redeploy it back into risk areas so you can take advantage of markets when they rebound.
5. Review your estate plan, ensuring all beneficiaries are who you still want them to be. I can't tell you how often an inlaw becomes an outlaw, and adjustments need to be made.
6. Evaluate your income tax return and upcoming financial matters that might impact your taxes to see if we need to activate a tax strategy for you.

So, I remember to touch on all these areas. I've developed a memory device to remind me to discuss assets, liquidity, income, growth, estate, and taxes. I call it "A.L.I.G.E.T."

J. BARRY WATTS

About the Author

J. BARRY WATTS
Founder, WealthCare Corporation

I've always been passionate about helping people. In the rural Ozark hills where I grew up, that might have meant taking food to a sick neighbor, helping the farmer down the road get his cows back inside the fence, or holding hands and praying with the one who'd just experienced a devastating loss or faced an excruciating decision.

Though my original credentials were in economics, my heart for helping seemed most fully expressed through the church. I became a minister to help enrich people's lives. That often involved money, which led me to seek out partners in the financial industry who helped me simplify the explanation of the complexities of money, taxes, and investments. Strategies developed within the financial realm eventually led to the establishment of WealthCare Corporation.

I went on to serve as a CERTIFIED FINANCIAL PLANNER™ and became credentialed to represent clients in front of the IRS. Over time, we've grown into a firm of professionals in an ecosystem of specialties, committed to helping people preserve and grow their wealth while creating a legacy for future generations.

We've learned to integrate tax strategy into the process of designing retirements and managing wealth. The work we do for clients centers on five building blocks — tax reduction, wealth management, risk protection, exit planning, and legacy design. All blend together to provide a personalized approach to lifetime wealth management, allowing people to retire comfortably, age with dignity, and create a legacy for generations.

Today, over thirty years after I began my journey, WealthCare Corporation is a national personal wealth firm serving individuals, families, and businesses who want a more customized approach. Unlike other firms, WealthCare Corporation is a personal wealth firm that takes a tax-centric approach to holistic, lifetime wealth creation, and preservation.

We are grateful for the opportunity to serve our customers and are passionate about our business. We believe tax strategy is personal, investment strategy is personal, and family legacy planning is very personal. And so, at WealthCare Corporation, we believe wealth advice should be personalized, allowing you to retire with confidence, age with dignity, and leave a lasting legacy for your family.

WealthCare

SPRINGFIELD
2847 S. Ingram Mill, Suite B 100
Springfield, Mo. 65804

Phone: 417.882.1726
Email: PriorityCare@WealthCareCorp.com
Web: WealthCareCorp.com

Made in the USA
Columbia, SC
27 June 2024

7c24c8f2-f495-4997-b4b3-256a0f448300R01